# Conten

# Introduction

This booklet was originally published by the Socialist History Society under the same name. I have added some items to the text, tidied up the references and issued the book as a second edition under my own self-published name. I would like to thank the SHS for bringing out the first edition and for their advice and guidance.

One of my many regrets in writing this history is that I left it too late. There are innumerable people who might have added colour to the perceptions contained in these pages. Growing up in Kirkby I was told that there was a man who lived on my road who had been a volunteer in the International Brigade. It was said that he had been put in front of a Francoist firing squad but had been spared at the last moment and had been left with a speech impediment as a result of this psychological injury. I was acquainted with Frank Deegan whose work is referenced in this history. He gave one of the few first-hand accounts of life in the CPGB in Bootle in the 1930s, followed by his experiences in the International Brigade. My dad Bill Jones, now deceased, was a joiner and a member of the Amalgamated Society of Woodworkers and was on first name terms with Leo McGree who he greatly admired. I was on nodding terms with Paddy McLaughlin, an Irish man who used to sell the '*Irish Democrat*' in Liverpool, the paper of the Marxist Connolly Association. His son went on to lead the British Movement, the most virulent Nazi organisation of the post war era.

All these people are now dead and gone. But among their children and grandchildren there will still be echoes of the struggles, the fears and the victories of the period.

Chris Jones,
August 2024
marmadukestreet2022@gmail.com

# Foundation: a party of a new type.

The reputation of Liverpool for political radicalism and trade union militancy is well known. In the 1970s and 1980s it was acquired as the result of political and industrial unrest which accompanied the seemingly relentless decline of the city's economic base. From the perspective of the 21st century it is hard to imagine Liverpool as anything other than a left leaning Labour Party stronghold. Conservative politics in the city are now, by and large, extinct. The history of Liverpool, as recalled by the leftish mind, is full of instances where the population stood up to authority and defended their often-meagre corner: city wide general strikes, gunboats on the Mersey, James Larkin and the repeated struggles of the unemployed are rightly advanced as evidence of the city's radical past. And prior to the first world war Liverpool was indeed to the fore during the industrial unrest which swept the country in 1911.[1]

However, although the citizens of Liverpool may have behaved radically in the streets, docks and factories, they voted conservatively at the ballot box. For almost a century from 1841 the city of Liverpool was Conservative. Even the expansion of the voting population to all men after the first world war and to women in 1928 did not shift the city's loyalty to the Conservative Party. On numerous occasions their candidates were elected unopposed in city wards. While other cities such as Glasgow elected avowedly socialist councils, Liverpool's radicalism expressed itself in direct action and not at election time.

While the first world war may have induced a truce in the pre-war industrial unrest, by 1918 some familiar notes were being sounded with new and serious outbreaks of civil dissent. In 1919 militant disobedience in Liverpool even spread to the police force who went on strike for the first time, occasioning military

---

[1] https://www.bbc.co.uk/news/uk-england-merseyside-14529243

intervention on the city's streets. Indeed, the end of the first war presented the civil authorities with a combination of factors which would all point in the direction of civil unrest. There was an influx of young men from the battle front in Belgium and France, trained in the use of arms and used to military organisation. This influx resulted in a rise in unemployment and a pool of disgruntled workers, denied any prospect of work. There was enormous poverty in the city and a patchwork of welfare facilities which proved wholly incapable of meeting the needs of the population. Across the sea in Ireland armed rebellion was well underway, a fact which would not have escaped people in some working class areas of Liverpool who regularly voted for Irish Nationalist candidates in local elections. In Russia meanwhile, the workers and soldiers had joined hands to exact their own demands at the point of a gun. Not far from Liverpool slow demobilisation of the armies led to riots among the allied troops[2] and there was the strong suspicion at the top of the military that Bolshevik ideas at the front had cost the forces dearly before and after the war had ended[3].

At this time of ferment, the forces of the left were undergoing a period of instability too. By 1918 the Labour Party in its modern form was only eighteen years old. Born from an amalgamation of more or less leftish streams of opinion in 1900 and emerging as an independent force from a previous loose alliance with the Liberal Party, the Labour Party began life in an era where large swathes of the working class had no vote, and all women of any class were denied this right. Its members advocated political ideologies ranging from gentle, reform-minded, morally inspired Christian Socialism to militantly atheistic Marxism. In the Independent Labour Party there were many who had refused to fight in the war and paid the price for their socialist principles by acting as

---

[2] Kinmel Park mutiny, March 1919
https://www.iwm.org.uk/collections/item/object/1030010079
[3] On 23 October 1924 it was reported in the *Liverpool Echo* that Major General Seely blamed Communist agitation for the success of the German advance in the 1918 offensive.

stretcher bearers at the front or, for the more uncompromising, enduring jail sentences [4].

By 1918 the Labour Party emerged from the wreckage of the conflict into a changed world. A widened electorate opened new prospects for the party. But the world had moved on since the gentle Socialism of the pre-war world. The war had brought the working class of Britain precious little to show for all their suffering. While the focus of the Labour Party may have been on electoral advance there were insistent voices on the left who argued the events in Russia had shown a more direct means of achieving socialist change than the rounds of political musical chairs played out in parliament. Across the world new forms of Socialism were crystallising which demanded and required revolutionary transformation of society, and these inspired huge numbers of people.

There had been people before the war who had not been satisfied with the menu for change offered by the reform minded leadership of the left in the UK. As ever in leftist politics these voices were split into fractious and mutually hostile groups. None of these groups were large, even if they were influential. Within their ranks there was frequently internal discord which would threaten to break out into further splits and factions.

Many of these groups sat outside the mainstream left but for our purposes the ones to focus on will be the British Socialist Party, the Socialist Labour Party and the shop stewards movement. The areas of disagreement inside and between these organisations included three important areas which would dominate the non-Labour left for subsequent decades. These were first, the attitude to be taken to working with the gradualist, reformist Labour Party. Second was the question of whether it was worth fighting for parliamentary representation. On this view any parliamentary route to social advance was an illusion. Third, the role of industrial struggle in advancing the interests of the working class.

Of these groups the British Socialist Party was already part of Labour's 'broad church' and had a similar organisational standing

---

[4] https://menwhosaidno.org/context/index.html

to the Fabian Society or the Independent Labour Party: part of the popular, diverse pageant which constituted Labour's ranks. The Socialist Labour Party and others preferred to stay aloof from the contaminating effects of the reformism they saw in Labour's parliamentary participation.

There were other currents of opinion which formed part of the left in the Liverpool of 1918. There had grown up in the war a vociferous shop stewards' movement. This was suspicious of promises made by career minded trade union or political officialdom. This was a movement which saw industrial action arising from rank-and-file activity as the surest route to economic liberation. There was a lively syndicalist current of opinion in Liverpool which looked for inspiration to American trade union activism, itself deeply suspicious of labour movement officialdom. Trans-Atlantic traffic and union activity among the seamen provided a ready source of syndicalist ideas. In 1920 the International Workers of the World ('Wobblies') had their own club in Byrom Street.

In Liverpool it was these three trends which formed the main body of opinion which, by the end of the second decade favoured the formation of a new Communist Party. The pressure of developments in the post war world, the intense gravitational pull of the events in Russia and the formation of the Third International made the creation of the new party ever more likely. This pressure overcame the traditional centrifugal force which caused the groups on the left to split into smaller organisations. By 1920 the tradition of fission on the left became one of fusion.

Thus it was with a sense of history in the making that numerous groups who had spent the previous decade in heated disagreement now came together, put aside their differences and joined forces. It was not so far-fetched to believe that the events in Russia would spark the sort of world changing transformation that occurred in the north of England just one hundred years before. The industrial revolution was, after all, almost within living memory, and one of its main arteries, the Liverpool Leeds canal ran into the heart of the city.

On 31st of July 1919 a Communist Unity Convention drew together many of the forces of the left to establish a 'party of a new type'. The largest of the component parts of the convention came from the British Socialist Party. In addition to their delegates came members from the Socialist Labour Party. Because, inevitably, there were splits within that party concerning the new Communist Party, only one faction attended. These were grouped with other left forces into an umbrella section called the Communist Unity Group (CUG).

The Merseyside contingent to the conference was composed of the following delegates. The Liverpool (East) branch of the British Socialist Party were represented by Mrs. Bamber, Mr. J. Goldstein and Mrs Walker. The CUG delegates from Liverpool were J. Hamilton and J. Morton. There was another delegate from the CUG listed for Birkenhead named J Fitton[5]. Of these delegates there are some interesting observations to make. Mrs Mary Bamber was a trade union activist and one of the first people in Liverpool to hold a Communist Party card. Her daughter Elizabeth was a regular attender at the Socialist Sunday School in Marmaduke Street, in the Kensington area prior to the foundation of the CPGB. This later became the address of what the *Liverpool Echo* later called a 'Communist Club'. Elizabeth also became a member of the Communist Party when she was eighteen.

In February 1922 Elizabeth, or Bessie as she was known, married the secretary of the Liverpool branch of the CPGB Mr Jack Braddock and they became one of the most powerful political unions in Liverpool's history. They came to dominate Labour politics in the city and as the century wore on, their views became more and more anti-communist. A statue of Bessie Braddock stands in Lime Street station. At the time of her marriage, Bessie was the treasurer of the nascent communist organisation.

---

5

https://www.marxists.org/history/international/comintern/sections/britain/subject/unity_convention/delegates.htm

Joe Goldstein, another delegate, remained in the Communist Party until he died in the 1970s. Mrs Walker is likely to be Mrs Annie Walker [*See biographical notes*].

It is hard to estimate how many people joined the new party in Liverpool. The British Socialist Party claimed a national membership of some 6000 people but James Klugmann considered their membership record keeping to be of poor quality with many members not even contributing their dues[6]. The Socialist Labour Party's main strength was in Scotland, and it is hard to know how many in Liverpool would have emerged from that organisation to join the CPGB or any of the other disparate groups and movements which came together at this point. Klugmann argued that the structure of the Communist Party around the foundation years resembled that of its largest component: the British Socialist Party. Alongside sloppy membership records came a federal structure: positions on the leading committees of the party were divided by region rather than suitability of candidates for leadership roles. By 1922 the requirement of the Comintern to professionalise the operation in Britain on Bolshevik lines led to new proposals for organisation in the form of a report by Harry Pollitt and R Palme Dutt. The proposals in the report were carried into policy at a congress in Battersea in 1922 and the organisational structure of the CPGB was in essence unchanged until the dissolution of the CPGB in 1990. One of the first tasks of the new organisation was to calculate how many genuine members it had. As soon as the new party began to keep accurate membership figures in the early 1920s the number was given as, roughly, 2000 nationally. The main strength of the new party was in London and Scotland. The rest of the membership, divided over Great Britain as a whole, must have meant that the party had very few members in Merseyside. The ramshackle organisational structure was not the only thing the CPGB inherited from its British Socialist Party roots. The British Socialist Party had been a party of meetings and

---

[6] James Klugmann, *History of the Communist Party of Great Britain, Vol 1,* Lawrence and Wishart, London 1968

propaganda mainly, with little emphasis placed on activism. Its paper, *The Call*, contained long, theoretical tracts and never achieved a

large circulation. After amalgamation, the name of the paper was changed to *The Communist*, but its tone did not substantially alter. In 1922 the paper was relaunched as the *Workers World* which in turn changed its name to the Workers Weekly. Both the *Workers Weekly* and *Workers World* little in the way of local coverage and their usefulness as a source of

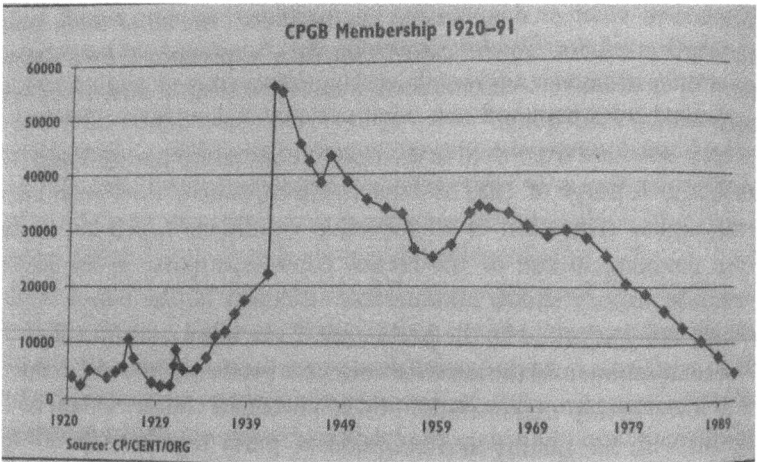

CPGB Membership 1920–91

*From 'Communists and British Society', Morgan, Cohen and Flynn, Orem Press, 2007)*

information about events on Merseyside is limited.

The Battersea changes introduced a structure in which the Central Committee (CC) implemented the policy of biannual congresses. A political bureau tweaked policy between CC meetings in the light of unfolding events. An organising bureau ensured that decisions of the CC were operationalised. Underneath the CC sat the District Party Committees (DPC).

The country was divided into ten districts, each obliged to conduct its own congress which would apply national policies to local conditions. Liverpool was considered a district and its first congress was on December 9, 1922. Decisions at DPC congresses would be binding on Local Party Committees (LPC). In 1924 the number of LPCs in Liverpool was given as 3. In 1925 this number was 4.

The party in Liverpool faced problems which were, in some respects, unlike the rest of the country. Although the city was large and its workers were living in often atrocious conditions, the composition of the workforce was different to other centres of militancy. The party saw itself as a party of the working class and the composition of the workforce therefore had very significant implications for its politics and activities. Nationally the party was strongest among workers in mining areas and in engineering. Anywhere where workers were congregated in large numbers became strongholds of communist organisation. The textile industry in Lancashire became a stronghold in the 1920s. But in the Liverpool of the 1920s such workplaces were unusual. Instead of the factories and the mines, Liverpool had the docks, the shipyards and the men who went to sea. There were also builders, but the casual and episodic nature of building and dock work and the months away from home at sea made solid industrial organisation in these fields very difficult for the party. Add to this the ever-present risk of becoming blacklisted as a militant and the difficulties multiplied. In 1932 the chief compiler of blacklists, the Economic League, held its annual conference in the city.[7]

In the inter war years there was one group who offered a constant source of activity and recruitment for the party: the unemployed. Permanently short of money the unemployed were also hard to organise but the CPGB's best activists brought to their organisation a sense of purpose that, for such a small organisation, was very impressive. Across Merseyside large numbers of unemployed responded to the call for 'Work or Full Maintenance', the slogan of the communist led National Unemployed Workers Committee Movement. In their book 'Communists and British

---

[7] *Liverpool Echo*, 2 May, 1932

9

*Society 1920-1921'*, Kevin Morgan and colleagues put the challenge facing the organisers of the unemployed like this:

*'Aneurin Bevan described it as a challenge of 'quite peculiar complexity' to attempt to give 'organisational expression to circumstances from which men are trying desperately to escape'*[8]

Some of the leaders of the unemployed workers, including Jack Nield in the early 1920s, could fall foul of draconian sanctions on their activities. Nield was deprived of benefits because, it was argued, his political activities on behalf of the unemployed precluded any genuine attempts to find work. And when unemployed demonstrations turned rowdy, it was disproportionately communists who paid the fines and, eventually, served the time.

Calculating the numerical strength of the party in Liverpool in the 1920s is not straightforward. There was the legacy problem inherited from the record keeping of the British Socialist Party to contend with. But even when this problem was resolved after 1922 any attempt at a headcount of Liverpool party members in the 1920s is complicated by the fact that it was possible for a time to be both a communist (small c) and a member of the Labour Party. Even membership of the Communist Party itself was tolerated as being compatible with Labour Party membership for a short period. After all, members of the British Socialist Party who had rubbed along in branches with Fabians and Independent Labour Party members would see little reason to change this situation just because their party had, arguably, simply had a change of name and joined with other more exotic strands of the Labour movement. In 1920 there was a porous wall dividing mainstream Labour and the communists. Even before the formation of the Communist Party there were voices in the Labour Party who argued that its broad-church approach was sometimes too broad to carry a consistent message. This relationship became increasingly uncomfortable for the Labour Party over the decade. Many in the new Bolshevist party, such as the Socialist Labour Party, had made

---

[8] Morgan K, Cohen G, Flinn A, *'Communists and British Society 1920-1991'*, Orem Press, 2007

an ideological point of telling the world that the Labour Party was a waste of working people's time and effort.

An example of the porous nature of the relationship between the Labour Party and the Communist Party came in November 1920, some three months after the foundation conference of the CPGB. In an article entitled '*Colonel Malone At The Stadium*' the *Liverpool Echo* reported that *''under the auspices of the Independent Labour Party'* Colonel Malone MP[9] had put to his audience '*whether parliamentary or Soviet action would be better for the country'*. Malone himself had said that '*he could but turn his feet slowly but steadily towards communism'* and he advised that where no communist was standing in an election, that a Labour Party candidate 'be sent in'[10]. Colonel Malone represented, on a national level, phenomena which were being played out in the branches of the Liverpool Labour Party. He was in his own right an example of how the left of the Labour Party and the communists were almost inextricably linked. A first world war air ace, he had been a Liberal Party MP and had written numerous tracts attacking the left. But after the establishment of the Soviet Union, he was taken on a tour of that country conducted by leaders of the revolution including Trotsky. On returning he became active in the 'Hands Off Russia' campaign and was jailed for a publication he wrote imploring members of the military to refuse to fight against the newly formed workers state. He joined the British Socialist Party and sat in Parliament as a Labour MP, becoming a Communist when the CPGB was formed. In that sense he was the first Communist MP. Other 'legacy' MPs followed who had been elected under the Labour banner but later identified as Communist.

It wasn't just the outpourings of maverick MPs which gave rise to discomfort in Labour about the communists in their midst. The communists claimed to be in Lenin's words, a 'party of a new type'. What reformists in the Labour Party now faced was not the fractious and disorganised voices of the pre-war left. Now they were faced with a party united under tight discipline which

---

[9] https://en.wikipedia.org/wiki/Cecil_Malone
[10] *Liverpool Echo*, 1 November, 1920

regarded itself as a single ideological unit. More than that, it now owed allegiance to an external authority in the shape of the Third (Communist) International. And this loyalty was not merely theoretical. Mrs Mary Bamber attended the congress of the Third International in 1920. The International would soon become known as the Comintern. Subsequent prominent members of the party would also visit Russia. In fact, the advice to British Communists from Lenin was precisely that they become active both in the Unions and in the Labour Party and, in his words, support the Labour Party '*in the same way as the rope supports a hanged man*'[11].

The members of the CPGB were organisationally and ideologically a very different proposition to the national Labour Party. In Liverpool the power and influence of the Catholic church was still an important feature of the local political scene, particularly among the part of the population who leaned towards Ireland. In the Liverpool of the 1920s it was still possible to vote for protestant candidates and Irish Nationalist candidates at local elections. Large swathes of the city had, for a generation, been where large numbers of Irish people had made their home in tight communities. The influence of the Catholic church was still enormous. The militant atheism of the CPGB would be a rare item that the opposing religious sectarian forces in the city could denounce in perfect unison. In the 1920s and early 1930s the CPGB was fierce in its denunciation of religion. The word that communist journalists consistently used when describing religion was 'dope'. The animosity was mutual, and a feature of election campaigns of the period were strident instructions from the pulpit to reject the option of a communist vote at the polls. In the 1930s

---

[11] VI Lenin *Left Wing Communism an Infantile Disorder,* 1920

the local Orange Order attacked and broke up Communist events with some regularity.

But perhaps the most significant area in which the Communist Party differed from the Labour Party was its emphasis on the importance of extra parliamentary and street activity. Serious independent electoral activity on the part of the CPGB did not really take off until the middle of the decade when the campaign of expulsions and proscriptions had more or less rooted the CPGB out of the Labour Party. The exception to this in Liverpool was in

St Annes ward in 1921. Here Jack Nield challenged local trade union and Labour grandee and devout Catholic James Sexton but was beaten by 57% to 43% of the vote. The following year he won the St Annes council seat, taking 57% of the votes, though this time against a different candidate.

The activity of communists on the ground may well have alarmed the Catholic minded, reformist leadership of local Labour. Although numbers were still low the members of the CPGB were highly motivated, well organised and ferocious in advocating for the rights of the post war working class in Liverpool. It was not difficult for the party to find causes to fight for. Unemployment was high, housing conditions were appalling, the health of the population had always been bad, but the privations of the war and, latterly, the Spanish flu had made new inroads.

Notwithstanding the low membership numbers, the CPGB initiated an ambitious campaign of meetings booked in large and prestigious venues. The difference between these and the 'Colonel Malone' meeting was that they were proudly under the auspices of the Communist Party. At these meetings national leaders of the party would outline the shape of the new party's thinking. At least four of these events were organised in 1921 and all were advertised in the *Liverpool Echo* . In the illustrated example above there was JE Hodgson, W Gee and FL Kerran representing the executive committee of the party. All three were old British Socialist Party hands who had migrated to the new party. Kerran would leave the CPGB when, in 1923, the Labour Party made dual membership of Labour and the CPBG a reason for expulsion. In the 1930s he was heavily criticised in the columns of the *Daily Worker*[12]. JJ Vaughan was the Labour mayor of Bethnal Green, now appearing on a Communist Party platform. This indicated that problems of dual identity were not confined to Merseyside.

In 1921 the CPGB had its own premises in Marmaduke Street, previously the home of the British Socialist Party, and it had an organiser by the name of Ieuan Peter Hughes. In April 1921 Mrs Bamber herself was in the chair at one of these rallies. In an article entitled '*Woman speaker's views at city communist meeting*' the *Liverpool Echo* report was so startled that they quoted Mrs Bamber in full:

*'Their policy was definite, founded on the complete overthrow of the capitalist system. There will be no doubt about the methods we mean to adopt to bring about that desire. It was decided yesterday...we will use every method to consolidate the power of the workers of this and other countries; legal if possible but illegal if necessary. Our aim is to destroy the whole system under which*

---

[12] *Daily Worker*, '*Mr FL Kerran was always an optimist*', 23 October, 1931

*we are living - that is the party message to the workers of this and other countries'*

By 1926 neither Hodgson nor Bamber were still in the party, for a differing reasons.

Apart from organising rallies the local CPGB threw themselves into an activity which would mark out their entire local interwar character: organising the unemployed. Local discontent over unemployment had by 1921 boiled over into civil unrest with one demonstration resulting in an impromptu occupation of the Walker art gallery. The resulting arrests captured much of the Communist Party leadership of the time. Jack Braddock, the secretary of the local district was arrested. John Nield, the St Anne's ward councillor was also arrested. Also arrested were George Garrett who went on to be a published working-class writer and was at this point still a communist, John Meehan who had been expelled from the USA for his revolutionary beliefs and John Flood, a Communist Party member. All five were bailed at the city magistrates on September 14, 1921.

'Over the water' in Birkenhead there had also been arrests in 1921. In April ironworker William Henry Bishop had been arrested at the Haymarket, a local 'speakers corner' and charged with making speech which was 'intended or likely to cause disaffection to his Majesty, to prejudice recruiting and to cause disaffection in the civil population'. He was released by the magistrates to the cheers of an awaiting crowd outside the court. The charge of making inflammatory or 'seditious' speeches was not an unusual one for members of the CPGB in the 1920s, locally or nationally. Many figures from all ranks of the party were prosecuted and many, including Colonel Malone, were fined or imprisoned for what they said or wrote. John Braddock, the secretary of the Liverpool Communist Party was arraigned before magistrates in April 1922 charged with using 'obscene language' after addressing a meeting of 300 dockers in Blundell Street. The accusation was denied. The charge was thrown out with the chairman of the bench 'leaving it up to the good sense of the defendant to avoid such language'. This might suggest some sympathy from the chairman. Mr CH Rouse had the same name as a CH Rouse who unsuccessfully stood for Labour in an 1891 election for the city's school board [13].

An interesting feature reported in 1922 was the existence in Liverpool of an 'Anti-Communist Party' which had an office in Castle Street. It is not clear what this organisation believed or what its activities consisted in and, letters in the *Echo* apart, there is little record of their existence. A letter was published in the *Echo* expressing thanks to the organisation for the charitable contributions they made to the correspondent, so perhaps its function was mainly dedicated to the relief of poverty. The only other time the Party appeared in the columns of the *Echo* was when they reported a fracas which took place between its officers in the headquarters of the Liverpool Distress Committee. A Mr John Wells was accused of attacking a Mr Henry Pitman over the disappearance of £50 from the account of the Anti-Communist Party. When it was put to Mr Pitman in court that the Distress League he worked for had four of its charity collectors in jail he was corrected by Mr Pitman who said it was only three[14]. More disturbing for the CPGB was the political career of a Mr D Prothero. He was reported to have attended a debate in the YMCA on Brownlow Hill in his capacity as 'a propagandist' for the 'Lancashire division' of the Communist Party. Ranged against him was a Mr JW Cherry speaking on behalf of the 'British Empire'. Mr Prothero laid out the case for Communism. But in the middle of the debate, he declared that he had changed his mind, was renouncing Communism and now saw Christian values as the way forward for humanity. In the 1930 local elections a Mr Dewi Prothero achieved 36 votes in Edge Hill standing as a Fascist [15].

In June 1923 an event took place which was to threaten the leadership of the new party in an entirely unforeseen way. It also

[13] *Liverpool Daily Post* Wednesday 18 November 1891

[14] *Liverpool Echo* '*Anti Communist's Dispute*' 4 September, 1922

[15]

https://en.wikipedia.org/wiki/1930_Liverpool_City_Council_election

indicated the way in which the affairs of the Liverpool Communist Party were shaped by the events to the west of the city in Ireland nearly as much as those in the USSR in the east. In a complicated and tangled sequence of events, the agreed facts as reported in the *Liverpool Echo* were these. Two men, James Phelan and John McAteer, planned to hold up a business on Scotland Road. In the end they attacked a post office. Two guns were carried to the raid. The eighteen-year-old son of the post mistress intervened during the robbery and was shot in the stomach. He died soon after. After these plain facts accounts start to differ. One of the robbers was cornered by a crowd outside the post office. The other disappeared. Under interrogation the cornered man, James Phelan, who gave his occupation as a blacksmith, said that he had received the guns used in the raid from Jack Braddock, the secretary of the Liverpool Communist Party. Phelan was convicted of the murder in July 1923 though it was accepted that he did not fire the gun. He was sentenced to death, but had his sentence commuted to life in prison. This left the question of Braddock and the supply of the guns to be resolved.

In November 1923 Braddock and another man, Augustine Power, were in court charged with supplying the fateful weapons. Braddock's case was that indeed he did know Phelan and had met him at the International Workers of the World (IWW) club in Byrom Street. Phelan had asked him and Power to look after some parcels. Braddock thought that the parcel he was given contained some papers and Power said that he was told that in his parcel were some tools Phelan needed for work. When someone came to collect the parcels on Phelan's behalf little thought was given to their contents and they were handed over. In fact, the parcels contained the guns and ammunition that were used in the raid. In this limited sense it was true that Braddock had 'supplied the gun'. In court Phelan, by now appearing as a witness for the prosecution, complained that the police had twisted his words about the June events and refused to answer any questions put to him by the prosecution counsel. As he was the only witness that the crown had to offer the case against the men collapsed and the judge stopped the trial. By 1924 both the Braddocks Jack and Bessie had left the CPGB.

Both Phelan and McAteer had interesting back stories of their own[16]. Portrayed in the *Liverpool Echo* as criminal desperadoes both were in fact Irish revolutionaries who had been involved in military activity in the civil war of 1922. It has been suggested that the action in Hopwood Street was part of a leftist inspired fundraising campaign for the Irish Citizen Army.

*Joe Phelan and John McAteer with others*
*In the above picture Jim Phelan on the steps of the Rotunda in Dublin...in the middle row dressed in a gaberdine and flat cap. McAteer is possibly the man in the hat on the extreme left (Courtesy of Andrew Lees, author of "Liverpool The Hurricane Port" [17])*

---

16

https://www.georgegarrettarchive.co.uk/component/content/article/2-uncategorised/73-jim-phelan-s-liverpool-home.html
[17] Lees A, *Liverpool The Hurricane Port* Mainstream Publishing, 2011.

McAteer managed to escape after the attempted robbery, which the *Echo* claimed had produced a mere four pounds. He fled to the Soviet Union where he was given a job in the port of Odessa teaching Soviet sailors. However, eventually he fell foul of the Stalinist purges of the 1930s and was shot as a spy in 1937.[18]

In June 1923 an advert appeared in the *Liverpool Echo* for a meeting in the Pudsey Street boxing stadium which gave an address where people interested in attending could apply for tickets. The address was in Kensington, at 14 Marmaduke Street. Marmaduke Street was the address given for the Socialist Sunday School which Bessie Braddock had attended. Mrs Braddock said in the joint autobiography she wrote with her husband Jack that it had been the Liverpool headquarters of the British Socialist Party. In the Liverpool street index of 1921, it is listed as belonging to the 'Socialist Democratic Party'. The same index gives William Mitchell as the secretary and Mrs Ellen Lowe as the caretaker. This owners name is likely to have been entered in error. No party of this name existed in Liverpool at the time. It probably refers to the Social Democratic Party. This organisation emerged after the Social Democratic Federation changed its name in 1907. The Social Democratic Party in turn changed its name following a conference in 1911 to the British Socialist Party. The 1923 and 1925 the street indexes gave the address to the Socialist Democratic Party, this time with Mrs Annie Walker as the secretary and Ellen Lowe still as the caretaker. This was also the address that had appeared in *The Communist* in January of 1923 in an article entitled 'Rebuilding the Communist Party". Articles appearing in the *Echo* described it as a 'Communist Club' throughout the 1920s[19]. Dave Cope of the 'Left On The Shelf' online bookshop lists Marmaduke Street as a possible address of the Communist Party bookshop for this period [20]. By 1927

---

[18] Barry McLoughlin: *Left to the wolves: Irish victims of Stalinist terror*. Irish Academic Press, 2007
[19] *Liverpool Echo 'Communist Activity'* 4 July 1927
[20] https://www.leftontheshelfbooks.co.uk/images/doc/Radical-Bookshops-Listing.pdf

Marmaduke Street was listed as belonging to the British Communist Party, with Mrs Walker and Mrs Lowe as its officers. The 1930 index names it as being the address of the Edge Hill Labour club, with Mr D Hornby as its secretary and with Ellen Lowe still hanging on as its caretaker.

On May 12 1924 the *Echo* reported events which took place in Seacombe which signalled the start of a sequence of events which occupied the CPGB's attention for many decades and still caused rancour fifty years later. Under the heading 'Poisonous Propaganda' the paper reported that a councillor in Seacombe had successfully passed a vote at the local Labour Party meeting to have CPGB members expelled from the branch in Wallasey and from the party as a whole. By December of that year the process of expulsions in Wallasey was complete. The following year the *Echo* reported that a letter from the District Organiser of the party, Mr Charles Hoyle, offering the services of the CPGB to Labour election campaigns in Wallasey and Liverpool had been rejected. Mr Barton for the Labour Party estimated the CPGB strength in Liverpool at that time to be about forty members[21].

# The Minority Movement in Liverpool

Nationally, the same theoretical problems which had troubled communists concerning the Labour Party also applied to work in trade unions. Was it possible to work in organisations whose main belief was in the perfectibility of society by gradual reform? Or was it necessary to build alternative organisations of the working class which would see the construction of a new social order arising out of the wilful destruction of the old? Initial attempts by communists to reforge the Labour Party, the political organisation of the British working class, from the inside met with failure after failure. The proscription of communists seemed to pick up pace in every sphere of the Labour movement becoming, in Noreen Branson's word, a 'purge' by the late 1920s. But in the trade

---

[21] *Liverpool Echo*, '*Poisonous Propaganda*' 12 May, 1924

unions the strategy of working within the established structures was more successful. Instead of advocating the establishment of new 'red' unions, as had happened elsewhere in Europe, the CPGB's efforts in the 1920s were to attempt to influence policy in the union movement from within. Building on rank-and-file efforts in the Miners Federation which pre-existed the party's own foundation, the party's industrial strategy focussed on the oddly named 'Minority Movement'. The aim of this movement was to coordinate left forces in the trade unions and to transform left wing minorities in the unions into majorities for resolute action. As such, the movement's name expressed confidence that such work within existing organisations could bring a positive result and was not a waste of time. Thus in 1924 the National Minority Movement was formed. Each industry had its own Minority Movement presence, although some industries were more Minority Movement minded than others.

The formation of the Minority Movement in Liverpool did not escape the attention of the right. In January 1926 John Tanner, the secretary of the United Empire League in the city (not to be confused with Jack Tanner, trade unionist [22]) specifically warned against the activity of the Minority Movement in the letters section of the *Liverpool Echo*[23]: *'It will be well for thinking members of the community to watch carefully the movements of the local Minority Movement'*. The letter pointed out that the leader of the local Minority Movement was the same as the local organiser of the Communist Party: Charlie Hoyle. It was not surprising for this local choice of Minority Movement secretary to be made. The national leadership of the Minority Movement closely overlapped with the leadership of British communism: Harry Pollitt, Arthur Horner of the South Wales miners and William Gallacher of 'Red Clydeside' were all key players in the organisation. One of the aspects of Communist Party work which both impressed and intimidated outsiders, depending on the observer, was the quality

---

[22] https://en.wikipedia.org/wiki/Jack_Tanner_(trade_unionist)
[23] *Liverpool Echo*, '*Ruling the Roost of Labour*' 2 January 1926

of Communist organisation. Bound by the Leninist doctrine of 'democratic centralism', once debate had ended decisions had been voted on it was the duty of all party members to fight for the policy in question. If the Minority Movement was led by communists, it was axiomatic that their policy would closely resemble that of the CPGB. But it would be a mistake to regard the Minority Movement as being the CPGB in trade union garb. The movement attracted, as it was intended to do, many workers who wished to see a stiffer resistance to the reductions in the standards of living of their class, without necessarily signing up to the entire programme of the CPGB. Nevertheless, the Minority Movement and its communist leadership were the subject of deep suspicion, sometimes with the flimsiest of triggers. While it was true that there were communists on many of the Lancashire Councils of Action during the General Strike of 1926 (six in St Helens, two in Garston and one in Bootle [24]), reports in the press exaggerated their influence to the point of hysteria. A report in the *Liverpool Echo* on May 25, two weeks after the General Strike, is typical. It informed the readership that a 'report', source unnamed, had been received which suggested that the Councils of Action set up by the TUC during the strike were in fact shadow Soviets intended to take over the running of the country in the event of a revolution. The report ended with an elegant example of how to conclude an article without necessarily standing by its contents: *'The local leaders of the Communist Party and the National Minority Movement were not to be found at their headquarters, but it is possible that the report may refer to some committee set up by them'.* The attempts of the Communist Party led National Unemployed Workers Committee Movement (later changed to the National Unemployed Workers Movement or NUWM) to gain representation on the Liverpool Council of Action during the General Strike were repeatedly rebuffed. The Liverpool Records Office holds a tetchy correspondence between the trade's council and prominent communist Jack Hedley where polite requests for

---

[24] Martin R, *'Communism and the British Trade Unions 1924-1933'* Clarendon Press, 1969

representation on the council were politely but resolutely declined [25].

On the 27th of June 1926, Tom Mann, hero of the Liverpool 1911 transport strike, addressed a Minority Movement meeting at the stadium in Pudsey Street. By August the *Echo* was coming to the opposite conclusion about Councils of Action that it came to in May: *'The formation on Merseyside of what is the be known as a Council of Action, representing approximately 100,000 members, will have the incidental effect of checking the influence sought to be exerted on trade unionists by the Communists'.*

While in other parts of the country the Minority Movement was establishing itself in a variety of industries, in Liverpool its

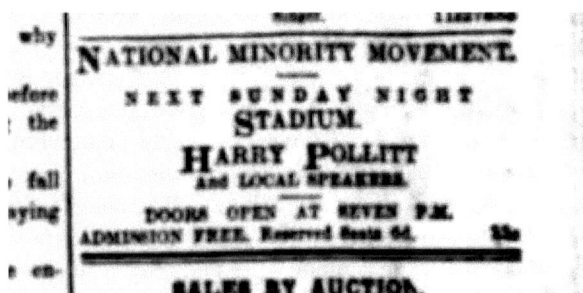

activity focused on the building industry, the docks, shipbuilding and among seafarers. In each of these industries separate rank and file newspapers were produced cheaply and sold to readers in the target trades. Building workers issues were addressed in *The Tin Can* and later *The Building Worker* but there were others. *The Hump* was aimed at Cammell Lairds workers and *The Dockers Bulletin* at the port workers[26].

It was not only in these large industries that the Minority Movement sought to operate. In August 'Jas Pearson' a Minority Movement activist defended the bar staff in Liverpool pubs who

---

[25] Liverpool Records Office 331 TRA/15/6/40-51
[26] Arnison, Jim *Leo McGree: What a man, what a fighter.*
Union of Construction and Allied Trade Technicians. 1980

had been accused of serving beer in dirty glasses. Addressing 'Froth Blower', the author of the letter of complaint in the *Liverpool Echo* , he wrote: '*Let Froth Blower examine the harassing conditions under which they (the bar staff) work i.e. short-handed, underpaid and long hours of employment. The remedy for dirty glasses is a larger staff, and the barmen should organise to bring this into effect'.*

The year 1925 began with a set of anti-communist letters in the *Liverpool Echo* . An unsigned letter 'To the editor of the *Echo* '' was published on Jan 2, 1925. It listed numerous organisations which had *'gone over to the Communist and Soviet cause'.* In an overheated diatribe against the Communist Party, the Minority Movement and the unions it pledged the loyalty of the new-born Fascist movement to authority: '*As an organised body ready to place themselves at the disposal of the authorities or, if necessary, to supplement their efforts and not as a band of irresponsible black shirted youths (sic), the British Fascisti certainly fill a gap, and are a necessity. Let us hope and pray they never need to be used'* By Jan 7 replies were published discounting '*the Fascistic, or should one say, Fantastic?*' version of British political life.

However, by April 1925 it became clear that the threat from the Fascisti was more than theoretical. On his way to address a meeting of the Minority Movement its general secretary Harry Pollitt, who went on to lead the Communist Party throughout the 1930s, was approached by men '*of the officer looking type*' according to Pollitt. They invited him to get off the train at Edge Hill, the stop before the Lime Street terminus, and go to address a meeting in Marmaduke Street. Sensing that the offer was not genuine, Pollitt refused. He was then manhandled off the train by a reported eight men. Pollitt appealed to a porter and a ticket collector for help and for them to call the police. Later, in their own defence, the railway workers said that the men told them that they were detectives and were taking an arrested man to an awaiting police car. Pollitt was then driven away and kept overnight at a Liverpool address, possibly to the Fascisti HQ 'in

Hotspur Street'[27] before being bundled into the car again and taken to a hotel in Wales. After an overnight stay the captive was put back into the car and was driven to Shrewsbury station and put back on a train, this time to London.

Reports of the kidnapping were delivered in a way which made the event sound lighthearted. The report in the *Echo* referred to it in its headline as a 'Kidnap Comedy'. And when the Home Secretary made a statement about the affair in Parliament there are frequent references to '(laughter)'. But to be fair, when the five men accused of the kidnap came to court Pollitt himself was inclined to see the funny side. He reported that they had brought him an eiderdown quilt and a cup of tea. One of his captors had 'rubbed his chest' with mustard and 'he did it very nicely', to laughter in the court. When he was offered the tea Pollitt said that he would drink it only if his captors drank it too (renewed laughter). However light-hearted his take on the events of his kidnap, it can only have come as a surprise to Pollitt that the jury accepted the Fascists' case that the kidnap had been nothing more than a 'prank' and a verdict of not guilty was delivered on the charge of kidnap.

# The bans and proscriptions in the Labour Party gather pace

For the Communist Party the news from Liverpool in 1925 was not encouraging. In October of the previous year the national conference of the Labour Party had declared that membership of the Communist Party was incompatible with membership of the Labour Party and that no communist should be supported at election time. This created problems for people who had been elected as Labour candidates who may have been members of one of the many organisations which formed part of the newly established CPGB. One such person on the national stage was

---

[27] *Liverpool Echo*, March 17, 1925

Shapurji Saklatvala. He had been a member of the Independent Labour Party up to the creation of the CPGB but had retained his Labour Party membership. He was the official Labour Party candidate in Battersea and won the seat joining another Communist, J Walton Newbold in Parliament on the Labour benches. In Liverpool, January 1925, this issue came to a head at a Labour and Trades Council rally in the stadium in Pudsey Street. In August 1924 Saklatvala had been booked by the Labour Party as a speaker ahead of their national conference in October. But by January 1925 opinion in the Labour Party had stiffened. Locally the Wallasey branch had already excluded Communist Party members in December. At the January stadium meeting the other speaker refused to share a platform with the communist Saklatvala. That speaker was Major AG Church. He had fought throughout the first world war and had received a DSO in the British intervention against the Russian revolution and in support of the White armies. It is tempting to speculate that this may have influenced his hard line in this case.

The looming confrontation at the national conference had local pre shocks. When asked by the *Liverpool Echo* about the position of Jack Nield, the Communist supporting Labour councillor in St Anne's ward, Mr WH Barton of the Labour Party declared that already Mr Nield was denied the Labour whip and was excluded from party meetings in the council.

The news from Liverpool for the communists did not improve later in 1925. In September 1100 delegates met in St George's Hall for the annual Labour Party conference. A proposal was put forward which would reverse the decision taken to exclude the CPGB. The proposal was one of the big events of the conference and many hard-hitting speakers were brought forward on each side. For the CPGB it was William Gallacher who led the charge. But for all his Clyde built eloquence the proposal to permit dual membership of the Communist Party and the Labour Party was decisively defeated. The *Liverpool Echo* described it as 'a rout'. The key issue which came up again and again was the attitude of the CPGB to constitutional and extra parliamentary activity. The Communist Party was accused of favouring violent change brought about by direct action in the streets, factories and barracks. This, it was argued, was incompatible with the gradualist and parliamentary route to reform favoured by the Labour Party.

After two crushing defeats it might be thought that the question would be settled. But the divorce between the two wings of socialist thought was messy enough to guarantee repercussions later on. In 1928 it was to re-emerge. As affiliated organisations, the trade unions had representation in the councils of the Labour Party. The Liverpool Trades Council (LTC), the overarching federation of unions and one of the oldest organisations of its type in the country, had direct input into the Labour Party. While communists were now barred from individual membership of the Labour Party it was not clear that TU branches and the Trades Council itself could not send communists to Labour Party policy events on their behalf as representatives. If they could not do so, would this not involve the Labour Party in interfering in the internal affairs of union branches?

On Jan 25, 1928, Luke Hogan, who was simultaneously president of the Labour Party in the city and of Liverpool Trades Council, wrote to the *Liverpool Echo* about an intervention at a meeting of the LTC by local Communist Party secretary and Amalgamated Engineering Union activist Charlie Hoyle. In his capacity as treasurer of the Liverpool National Unemployed Workers Committee Movement (NUWCM) Hoyle was attempting to get the LTC to insist on a raise in the rates of unemployment relief awarded by the local guardians. In a letter to the *Liverpool Echo* Hogan argued that the LTC had included Hoyle in the delegation to meet the Guardians 'under a misapprehension'. It was his duty to rule that Hoyle's eligibility to be an official delegate was invalid, he said, because members of the Communist Party were not entitled to any official position in the Labour Party or the LTC. In reply to this letter Charlie Hoyle argued that the decision of the Labour Party conference to exclude Communists was a recommendation only. He argued that his position on the LTC was as a representative of the Amalgamated Engineering Union (AEU) and the NUWCM, not of the Communist Party. He further argued that the reason that he was to be excluded was

because the Labour Party under Hogan's leadership had little stomach for the fight for more relief for the unemployed.

For the CPGB the deteriorating situation caused alarm and in September 1928, the issues at stake were once again thrashed out in the letters column of the *Echo*. Leo McGree, who became the most noted Communist in Liverpool of his generation, Charlie Hoyle and HS Martin had been expelled as delegates from the Trades Council on the grounds that they were members of a proscribed organisation. The case that they put in their letter was that the crushing defeat they had faced at the Council (115 votes to 33) represented the views of the delegates only and not of the working class at large. Further, they argued that as many of the big unions who carried large votes at the LTC met very infrequently, they could hardly even be said to represent their members. They concluded their letter by arguing that their expulsion was a fig leaf to disguise the fact that nationally the reformists were 'pursuing a policy of class collaboration with minimum resistance'. The response of Alderman Luke Hogan was swift. He argued that a challenge to the legitimacy of the delegates to the LTC who had expelled the Communist Party delegates, and the doubt cast on their right to represent their union branches was ironic from delegates whose loyalty was to the central committee of the CPGB and through them to the Comintern in Moscow.

The character of Luke Hogan is an interesting one in the history of Communism in Liverpool. He led the faction in the Labour Party nicknamed by some the 'Catholic Caucus' and by others the 'Red Flag-Shamrock' After Irish independence had been achieved most Irish nationalist opinion in Liverpool transferred to the Labour Party. The Irish Nationalist Party itself became the Catholic Party which in turn became the short-lived Centre Party but most working-class Catholics followed Luke 'the iron duke' Hogan and his leadership of the Labour Party. Some sixty years later Liverpool CPGB social historian Tony Lane would argue that Hogan and his followers had a firm ideological intent: *'Labour absorbed councillors who had been instruments of the church and it inherited organisations that knew more about clientism, autocracy and priestly patronage than about beliefs in democratic and constitutional procedures which were the hallmarks of the Labour Party and the 'respectable' working class. Although the Labour Party was now much larger, it was in practice two parties and the Catholic section, organised as a caucus, was dominant*[28]

The tone of the hostility to the presence of the CPGB on the left can be judged from yet another letter published in the *Echo* on March 6, 1929. Responding to an offer from the Communist Party to help in the Labour Party 1929 election effort in the Scotland division of the city, Davie Logan, who went on to be a Labour MP, rejected the offer out of hand. Speaking of the Communist Party supporters who might engage in the election he said: *'We are accustomed to seeing Lascars [Seamen of Indian origin] and coolies in 'The Paddy's Market' but it is rather unique to find them in the principal streets and preparing for an election in the Scotland division'.* These remarks were the more uncomfortable given that unpleasant race politics were a frequent background hum in Liverpool in this period. Ten years before this election a black citizen, Charles Wooton, had been killed by a white mob in the city. This was not an isolated event, with many of the city's minorities coming under attacks from bigots. In reply to Logan, Charlie Hoyle, describing himself now as the Sub District organiser of the party argued that *'He declares that the Communist Party and the lascars are 'alien to our people' indicating a splendid example of Labour imperialist psychology .... The presence of Lascars at a Communist meeting proved their willingness to unite with Liverpool seamen in opposition to the employers (our people) who use the colonial people as cheap labour'*

The expulsion of the Communist Party from the main Labour Movement organisations on Merseyside meant that the party was free to put its own agenda to the electorate. It is perhaps one of the greatest ironies of the party's history that, in its first decade, so much ink was spilled in debating whether or not to affiliate to the Labour Party and whether the passage to Socialism was possible

---

[28] Belchem J (ed) *'Liverpool 800'*, Liverpool University Press 2006.p43

through Parliament. By the end of the 1920s affiliation to the Labour Party was removed as an option by the Labour Party itself. The question of a parliamentary majority legislating Socialism via a communist presence also became academic. At every opportunity the electors in the city gave the CPGB a firm refusal. John Nield, the 'legacy communist' who had been elected on the Labour ticket before the ban, took a mere 0.8% of the vote in 1926. While the Communist Party's brightest star, Leo McGree took a mere 3% in a council by election in the Edge Hill ward in 1928. When the seat was up for election again later the same year, he got 2%.

The Communist Party, so frequently accused in the 1920s of not believing in constitutional and parliamentary means to achieve its goals, would go on to show an almost touching faith that the effort spent in fighting elections was worthwhile. In the almost certain expectation of humiliating defeat, they would, again and again, throw themselves into election after election as though there was a genuine prospect of winning. In the years to come, Leo McGree's 3% would come to be regarded as a good result.

# New times and the 'New Line'

Towards the end of the 1920s, political debates far away led to policies being adopted which would nearly wipe out the Communist Party in Liverpool. In 1927 the Comintern in Moscow changed the line of thinking of the world communist movement. This saw the introduction of a new sectarian turn in communist politics: the so-called 'Class Against Class' period. Instead of co-operating at rank and file level with people in other parties, a new hostility developed to people perceived as peddling 'dope' (a word which appeared regularly in the headlines of the *Daily Worker* in the early 1930s) about the possibility of reform under capitalism. Pedlars of these delusions were seen as useless enablers of a broken system and were actively holding back the working class. They put illusions into the minds of the workers that capitalism *'would wind itself up on request'*. Reformist dope pedlars offered the working class a national solution to their problems based on the friendly cooperation of classes. This led the Communist Party to characterise this trend of thinking as 'social fascism'. Throughout the pages of the *Daily Worker*, launched in 1930, this line of thought was very noticeable and in 1930 it was at its height. Indeed, the cooperation offered to the government by many in the leadership of the Labour movement with wage freezes, dole cuts and 'rationalisation' of industry gave some credibility to these views. Discussions with ICI chief Alfred Mond concerning how to shake out unnecessary workers in 'over-manned' industries at the same time as restraining the pay of those left became known as 'Mondism'.

Some historians of the CPGB have argued that the 'new line' was imposed on the party and represented the long arm of the Comintern reaching into British labour movement politics. Others have argued that although the policy may have originated in the USSR it landed on fertile ground in the UK. Disappointment with the first Labour government, outrage at the result of the general strike and the participation of Labour in the dole cutting national government meant that feelings on the far left were running high. The membership in the locals took little encouragement to regard the likes of Ramsay MacDonald as being worse than useless. In his pitch for the nomination of the Amalgamated Society of Woodworkers to be a delegate to the TUC congress of 1930, Leo McGree summed up these feelings in one sentence. He said he would *'fight against Mondism, rationalisation and the Social Fascist policy of the Labour Party'*[29]. First hand documents from Liverpool Communist Party for this period are hard to find, but there is a hand typed document dated April 6, 1929, in the archive of the People's History Museum in Manchester. It is the minutes of a party aggregate held to discuss 'The Right Danger in the Party'. The contents of the minutes reveal how popular the new line was in Liverpool. There is pronounced criticism of the organisation of the 10th Communist Party congress, before and after it took place. It is also highly critical of the leadership of the

---

[29] *Daily Worker*, March 8 1930 page 5.

party. The 10th congress in January 1929 saw an attempt to row back on some of the excesses of the Class Against Class line. This was the danger referred to in the calling of the aggregate in April. The member opening up the debate, Edmund Frow, said *'The majority of our EC have been divorced from the workshop for years. They should be sent back into the workshop where they could be of great value to the party'.* One JR Longworth said: *'In the party there is not democratic centralism, there is a central bureaucracy. This is expressed all through the party. Organisers think in terms of jobs'.* At the end of the meeting a resolution was composed summarising the views of those present. It was carried unanimously [30].

The result of the adoption of the 'Class Against Class' policy outlined above meant that the miniscule Communist Party in Liverpool had opened up a war on numerous fronts. Potential allies were treated with scorn. Unnecessary attacks were made on people who in other circumstances might have been able to support the claims of the working class. Not surprisingly, the effect of this sectarianism was to isolate the party. Party membership figures started to decline. From a figure of 385 members in the city in 1927 the Liverpool Communist Party showed a steady decline throughout this period. By 1930 the figure stood at 58 members[31]. An undated document entitled 'Draft resolution re the organisation of the Lancashire District of the CPGB " exists in the CPGB archive in Manchester at the People's History Museum Labour History Archive. It refers to the *'recent Meerut events'* which places it post 1929 and pre-1933, probably 1929. This document gives the entirety of Lancashire a membership of 550, and the document states that only 30% of these members could be

---

[30] Labour History Archive and Study Centre: CP/LOC/NW/3/02

[31] Worley, Matthew (1998) *Class against class: the Communist Party of Great Britain in the third period, 1927-1932.* PhD thesis, University of Nottingham.

considered active [32]. In July 1931 the Liverpool District declared that it would aim for a figure of 200 members which, said the *Daily Worker*, would be an increase of 104 members[33]. This would mean that the membership number in 1931 was 96. In declaring its aim to increase its membership the struggling party indicated where it saw its strength and where it perceived its priority areas for recruitment. The article in the *Daily Worker* said that it saw members coming from dockers (50), seamen (20), engineers (10), railwaymen (10), building (10), various (4). The same article accounted for the serious loss of members suffered over the previous years as being due not to the arid landscape of their sectarian policies. Rather it saw the problems as being due to the absence of social activities and party training.

# Organising the CPGB: members, officers and offices.

The reason that Bessie Braddock gave for quitting the CPGB in 1924 was that her hostility to paying the full-time officers of the party a too generous salary made her unpopular with party HQ. In the joint autobiography she wrote with Jack Braddock she said that the cutting of the salaries to 60% of its previous level was an achievement that she claimed for herself[34]. Whether this was the rate of pay of the national officers or of the local officials is not clear. And she does not say in her autobiography the figure that her efforts resulted in.

Whether the Liverpool district employed full time officers, what their pay was and the dates on which one succeeded another is difficult to determine. While the local party, at district congresses and in the party press, would give chapter and verse about its policies and opinions it was coy about its own internal

---

[32] Labour History Archive and Study Centre: CP/LOC/NW/3/02

[33] *Daily Worker*, 3 July 1931

[34] Braddock B, Braddock J, '*The Braddocks*' Macdonald, 1963

organisation. It requires some guesswork to construct a picture of who ran the party and when, and the number of members who were in the party they ran. But there are some points that can be made about party organisers and party organisation. Liverpool was regarded as both a 'district' and a 'local' in this period. Frequently the terms 'district' and 'sub district' were applied to the organisation. The likelihood is that Liverpool was a sub district of the Lancashire organisation. As a sub-district it took in Southport, Birkenhead, Liverpool and Crewe. From 1930 on the *Daily Worker* advertised events in the city as being under the heading 'Liverpool District'. But then, they refer also to the 'Birkenhead District' too so it is likely that they were referring to geographical areas and not party structures. In the mid 1930s both Liverpool and Birkenhead began to appear under the heading Lancashire and Cheshire District in the What's On adverts in the paper. In Merseyside itself the branch structure seems to be that in the late 1920s and early 1930s there were four 'locals': Liverpool Central, Edge Hill, Clubmoor and Birkenhead. At some point in the mid 1930s the branch structures seem to have been rationalised and are referred to as Liverpool North, East, Central and 'South End'. They also start to be referred to as 'branches' in the *Daily Worker* with reference to Everton, Exchange and Kirkdale branches in the late 1930s.

| Date | Name of Liverpool organiser | Source | Members |
|------|------|------|------|
| 1920 | Ieuan Peter Hughes | | |
| 1925 | Charlie Hoyle | Letter, *Liverpool Echo* | 40 members (*Echo* Oct 22) |
| 1927 | Charlie Hoyle | | 150 members (*Echo* July 4) |
| | | | 385 (Worley 1998) |
| | | | 104 members (*Echo* Sept 29) |
| 1930 | | | 126 Members (Worley 1998) |
| | | | 58 members (Worley, 1998) |
| 1931 | | | 94 members (*Daily Worker* July 3) |
| 1935 | Alec Hermon | *Daily Worker* | |
| 1936 | Frank Bright | Letter, *Liverpool Echo* | |
| 1938 | Jim Grady | *Daily Worker* | |
| 1939 | Frank Bright becomes Lancs district organiser | | |

It is difficult to pin down precise dates at which the district organisers posts were handed over and sometimes the most reliable way to determine dates is to use their signatures in letters to newspapers as a (unreliable) guide. Jim Grady is first described as a district organiser in the *Daily Worker* in 1938, though he signed a condolence letter to Alec Hermon in 1935. He replaced

Frank Bright in the post who went on to become Lancashire organiser in 1939 [35], taking over from William Rust.

Four successive Liverpool district organisers of the CPGB, Hoyle, Hermon, Bright and Grady went to the International Lenin School in Moscow in the early to middle 1930s: Charlie Hoyle and Frank Bright may well have been in the same 1930-1932 cohort. Alex Hermon attended in 1932-1935. Grady's dates are given as 1932. This might mean that he completed his studies in one year, or that he came home early. Hoyle was the youngest in the group while Bright was the oldest. Three were members of the party's central committee [36]. The sending of so many activists to Moscow over such a short time caused some controversy at the top of the Communist Party. Harry Pollitt, in particular, was bothered by the vacuum this might leave in the party's localities:

*'He also bridled at the removal of the erstwhile Liverpool and Manchester party organisers, Charlie Hoyle and Frank Bright, whom he strongly objected to remaining for the longer 'basic' course. In Hoyle's case, there was the additional consideration that his wife had succumbed to Graves' disease and was reported to be in an 'extremely worried and nervous condition'. Nevertheless, Hoyle did not return early, though he was given a partial release to work for the Comintern, and the only hope held out for his wife was to be found some factory work in Moscow.*[37]

The new sectarianism of the Class Against Class period coincided with and was the result of changes in the politics of the USSR. The principal of the Lenin school up to 1929 was Nicolai Bukharin, the veteran Bolshevik leader and leading figure in the

---

[35] https://grahamstevenson.me.uk/2008/09/19/frank-bright/
[36] McIlroy J, McLoughlin B, Campbell A, Halstead J, *'Forging the faithful The British at the International Lenin School'* Labour History Review, Vol. 68, No . I, April 2003
[37] Cohen G, Morgan K, *'Stalin's Sausage Machine. British Students at the International Lenin School, 1926–37'*, *Twentieth Century British History*, Volume 13, Issue 4, 2002, Pages 327–355,

Comintern. He was replaced at the ILS by Bela Kun, a Hungarian communist and enthusiast of the new line. Throughout this period in the USSR and the Comintern the early effects of the Stalinisation of international communism were becoming more pronounced. Both Bukharin and Bela Kun ended their lives in 1938 in front of one of Stalin's firing squads. It is hard to imagine what the experience of the school brought to the practice of these district organisers in Liverpool or what, in the end, they made of the deaths of these erstwhile revolutionary heroes.

While the deaths of Bukharin and Bela Kun might have been too distant from life in Liverpool to cause many ripples there was one death which, though it went unreported in the *Daily Worker*, must have given Frank Bright and Charlie Hoyle pause for thought, not that they are on record as saying anything about it. In the same years as they were at the International Lenin School there was another student there called Rose Cohen. Rose, who had been a suffragette before the first world war, was a full-time worker for the party and a foundation member. By the time she enrolled at the ILS she had done several dramatic and risky missions for the Comintern. A photograph of her exists in the People's History Museum in Manchester inscribed by Harry Pollitt: '*Rose Cohen – who I am in love with, and who has rejected me 14 times.*'[38]

She stayed on in the USSR after her time in the ILS, got married and had children. When Bright and Hoyle returned to England, she went on to edit the influential English language newspaper Moscow News. Perhaps she came to know all the British students at the ILS. The British community in Moscow could not have been very big in the 1930s. But by 1937 the mood in Moscow was considerably sourer as the full weight of Stalin's malice bore down. She was accused of spying for Britain, of being a British agent and, after a twenty-minute trial, she was convicted and shot the same day. Nobody in the Communist Party mentioned the fact, let alone protested. In 1958, two years after Khrushchev's 'secret' speech, Harry Pollitt enquired about her fate to the Russian authorities. They rehabilitated her and declared her a victim of

---

[38] https://en.wikipedia.org/wiki/Rose_Cohen_(feminist)

political repression. One is entitled to wonder what Bright, Grady and Hoyle made of these events.

The 1930s started with leaders of the Communist Party in Liverpool and in Birkenhead getting into trouble once more for seditious speeches. One member, Nugent Coffey, a communist then living in West Kirby, was prosecuted for speeches he made in the Haymarket, Birkenhead. He was prosecuted for making a speech which was described in court as being *'scurrilous, filthy...blasphemous and obscene'* although the words quoted from his speech to a modern ear, sound mild. The heart of the complaint against him was that his meeting outside the park gate in Birkenhead had become rowdy after one of his speeches. He had argued that 'the financiers' could get rid of the royal family any time they wanted 'as they had done in Spain'. This apparently enraged the crowd and led to the disorder of which he was accused[39].

The police didn't have it all their own way with street corner speakers. In 1932 the *Echo* reported that Nugent Coffey had himself taken out a private prosecution against a police inspector who had knocked him off the chair he was using to address a crowd. The inspector had forbidden the meeting to go ahead, though such open-air meetings had been held there 'for years'. When Coffey asked what would happen if the meeting went ahead the police inspector said that he *'would have to take the consequences"* but Coffey said that he didn't expect being pushed off the chair and into another man to be one of those consequences. The magistrate's chairman said that he didn't think the court would issue a summons. Coffey asked the court if there was a higher court he could apply to. When he didn't get a satisfactory response, he began to present an argument about the unfairness of the decision. He was invited by the chairman not to thump the witness box. *'Very well'* he replied *'we will give this due publicity'*

The glare of 'Class against Class' politics was not exclusively turned on people outside of the Communist Party in Liverpool. There was considerable highly critical attention turned on figures

---

[39] *Liverpool Echo* April 2, 1932

and organisations inside the party itself. Week after week the Liverpool organisation was subject to strident, public admonishment in the pages of the *Daily Worker* . In May 1930 Liverpool's effort in support of the *Daily Worker* revealed a *'sluggardness (which was) simply disgraceful'*. Liverpool was described as a 'black spot' for sales. This was in the same year as Leo McGree had his unemployment benefit stopped because he was caught selling the *Daily Worker* outside the Unemployment Assistance Board. McGree was the leader of the NUWM in Liverpool throughout this period. Week in and week out the criticism of the Liverpool Communist Party continued. The Liverpool members did not sell enough papers. They did not send in enough money for the fighting fund. They did not put enough adverts in the 'What's On' section of the paper. The Merseyside party was accused in 1931 of 'lagging behind' in failing to meet recruitment targets. In February 1930 the *Daily Worker* reported that the previous district organiser of the party in the city, Charlie Hoyle, had achieved over 10,000 votes in his attempt to become the leader of the AEU. At the age of 28, this was a notable achievement. But by April of the year William Rust would declare in the *Daily Worker* that all party members should *'join this fight against deviations from the correct Bolshevik line'* in the unions. He gave as an example of one of these deviations the story of a party member (possibly Hoyle himself) who was on the district committee of the AEU in Liverpool. This member had defied a party decision that he should speak at a meeting of striking engineers, wanting instead to wait for an invitation from his union to speak. This was *'trade union legalism with a vengeance'* according to Rust.

In 1932 the chorus of criticism reached a crescendo when the *Daily Worker* published a large article attacking the local party[40]. So bad was the impression of party life in the city that the central committee sent a commission to investigate matters and report. Under a disturbingly Stalinist headline which read *'Liverpool is now liquidating its unsatisfactory past'* the article about the report

---

[40] *Daily Worker* March 3 1932

opened with: *'The Liverpool district has for a long period been one of the weakest districts in the party'*. It continued: *'Some of the outstandingly bad features of our party in Liverpool were the social composition of the membership and the character of activities'* in other words, there was a problem with who the members were and what they did. The report said that the party contained too many unemployed and the membership would rather loll around in the party premises than engage with the working class. Later in that year the central committee would have reason to rethink their unkind conclusions.

In September of 1932 there was a serious outbreak of rioting in Birkenhead [41]. Successive large demonstrations of the unemployed led by the NUWM had failed even to get a hearing from the local councillors who set the rate of the dole for the area. Finally, a meeting took place where unemployed representatives including communists Leo McGree and Joe Rawlings saw local councillors pass a resolution demanding that the National Government abolish the means test. At the same meeting a conservative member of the Public Assistance Committee, the body who determined local benefit rates, made allegations that the unemployed were living the high life on dole money and spending their benefits on drink and gambling. When the crowds outside heard this, they went in great numbers to the councillor's house and a four day rampage ensued. Police violence, looting, indiscriminate arrests, revenge attacks and window smashing took place over an entire weekend. When the unrest had died down Joe Rawlings and Leo McGree were both arrested and charged with incitement to riot. Days later In Liverpool a demonstration of the unemployed led to similar ugly scenes involving baton charges and stone throwing. The main focus of the unrest in Liverpool was Islington Square, the traditional starting and end point of demonstrations in the city. When the dust had settled on the day's mayhem in the square arrests were made. The list of the arrested resembled the attendance register of the Liverpool Communist

---

[41] An excellent account of these events is given in Stephen F Kelly's *'Idle hands, clenched fists'* Spokesman books, 1987

Party district committee: Charles Heaton, Jack Hedley, Albert Cole, IP Hughes, and Fred Gibson were all among those charged, mostly for disorderly conduct. Over the water, Rawlings and McGree were sentenced to 20 months in prison. Another party member over there, Syd Greenwood aged 20, was sent to prison for one year. In Liverpool, Hedley got 9 months. Three of the Islington accused were found not guilty, but many others were bound over for one year and three got 2- or 3-months prison. Most of the evidence brought against the Islington accused was based on police eyewitness accounts. A notable feature of the trial was that one of the accused, Jack Braddock, now a Labour councillor, had some 19 police eyewitnesses testify against him. They swore they saw him on a lorry inciting riot. But Braddock was able to show that he was in fact at a meeting on council business at the time the rioting occurred, and he supported his case by producing numerous witnesses of his own, including members of other parties and a clergyman. Police witness mistaken identity caused the case against Braddock to collapse in, what the judge described as, 'the most complete alibi ever brought forward in a court of law'. But the now established unreliability of the eye witness testimonies did not help his fellow accused [42].

In the space of nine months the Merseyside Communist Party had gone from being severely criticised by the Party leadership for inactivity and being over-represented among the unemployed to having much of its leadership imprisoned for leading unemployed protests. Even now, the criticism did not falter. On December 5, 1932, the fighting fund column reported that: 'The districts showing a decrease (in contributions) are Birmingham, Liverpool and Bradford. In Liverpool most of the leading members are in jail and, as a result, the district is disorganised to a large extent'. Not large enough to spare the remaining members public criticism it seemed.

In the wake of the verdicts the CPGB on Merseyside embarked on a new field of activity. From early 1933 meetings were

---

[42] *Liverpool Echo* '*KC and the alibi. 'Police blunder lamentable'...Verdict that would be a mockery*' 28 Oct 1932

advertised in the *Daily Worker* for the organisation International Labour Defence (ILD). In January 1933 the first of the ILD meetings took place in Vittoria Street, Birkenhead. Considering the imprisonment of Rawlings and McGree, this was a natural place to found the ILD local. The advertised speakers were Arnold Ward, described as a 'negro worker' and C Boggild of the Independent Labour Party. Arnold Ward was a Barbadian communist and a founder of the 'Negro Welfare Association'. Fellow members included Jomo Kenyatta [43]. Boggild was the man on the lorry at Islington who the police 'mistakenly' took for Jack Braddock, though he was never charged. Frequent meetings were held in Liverpool and Birkenhead for the ILD, itself by now a proscribed organisation in the Labour Party. The years campaigning culminated in a rally at Picton Hall which attracted a crowd estimated by the *Daily Worker* as 1,500, with 500 outside the building. The cause of this surge of interest was not just the presence of Tom Mann on the platform. The news from Germany about the Nazi repression of opposition and in particular, the decapitation of the German Communist Party revealed that there were far more labour leaders to be defended.

Leo McGree

In April 1934 Leo McGree was released from prison. The *Daily Worker* claimed that 2000 workers came to meet him at Lime Street station. By now the activists imprisoned after the events in Birkenhead and Islington were all out of jail and the leadership of the party in the city was once again reconstituted.

## No Pasaran: The fight against Fascism in Liverpool

The CPGB in Liverpool were in the field early in the fight against Fascsim. In 1931 Oswald Mosley left the Labour Party and formed the New Party. It would be one year later that he united the small fascist parties in Britain into the British Union of Fascists (BUF). One of the first public events organised by the New Party

---

[43] https://en.wikipedia.org/wiki/Negro_Welfare_Association

in 1931 was a rally in Liverpool's boxing stadium in Pudsey Street. One of the speakers at the event was John Strachey who, after renouncing Mosleyism, was later to become a feature writer for the *Daily Worker* . The meeting was subjected to sustained heckling from the crowd which included many Communist Party members, who, according to the *Daily Worker*, challenged the speakers to debate with the Communist Party the proposition: *'That the New Party was a fascist party with the usual fascist programme'*. The meeting ended with a section of the audience 'giving three cheers for the Soviet Union' and singing The Red Flag.

As the 1930s wore on anti-fascist activities took more and more of the attention of the party and frequently ended in violent confrontations on the streets. Charlie Martinson and John Flood (last mentioned in the Walker art gallery 'siege' of 1921) in Bootle refused to be bound over by a court which found them guilty of causing affray at a BUF open air meeting. Martinson would later go on to fight fascism in Spain. Nugent Coffey from Birkenhead, who had previously been prosecuted for making seditious speeches, in 1934 organised a bike ride from Liverpool to a large anti-fascist rally in Belle Vue, Manchester. By the end of 1934 and the start of 1935, the fear of rising fascism led the party in the city to take the first steps toward a tolerance of difference between opponents of the fascist tide. In November 1934 the *Daily Worker* reported a meeting in a church community hall in Hope Street which passed a resolution calling for the release of Ernst Thaelmann, the leader of the German Communist Party. But on the streets the atmosphere was getting worse and worse. Supporters of the 'Greenshirts', members of the leftish Social Credit Party[44] were attacked in Church Street along with *Daily Worker* sellers. There was fighting at a large Fascist meeting in the city which was being addressed by the maverick Major General

---

[44]

https://en.wikipedia.org/wiki/Social_Credit_Party_of_Great_Britain_and_Northern_Ireland

JCF Fuller[45] noted occultist and fascist fellow traveller. In 1936 there were repeated attacks on Communist Party and NUWM meetings and street activities in the Scotland Road area by Orange Order 'Ironsides' activists which resulted in numerous prosecutions[46].

By 1936 the self-indulgence of the Class Against Class period had run its course in the face of fascism's existential threat to democracy. In 1933 the *Daily Worker* could write an article entitled 'Maxton's fancy picture of the struggle in Germany destroys workers unity' about leftist Red Clydesider James Maxton MP. By March 1937 the *Liverpool Echo* would advertise a rally with Maxton and Harry Pollitt the headline acts. In October of that same year Oswald Mosley attempted to visit Liverpool again. As he got up to speak, he was met with a shower of missiles thrown by the crowd, one of which wounded his head. Frank Bright wrote to the *Echo* to distance himself and the party from accusations that the Communist Party were behind the fracas[47]. The fascist paper *Action* was not convinced. Its front page declared '*Mosley struck down by red curs*'[48]

## The Popular Front on the Mersey

In the early 1930s the CPGB had pursued a policy of 'united front from below'. In reality this meant that the CPGB would cooperate with members of other parties who were willing to criticise their own party, trade union or social movement leadership. This made attempts at unity half-hearted to say the least. In May 1932 a report appeared in the *Daily Worker* which warmly recounted that '*there was determined opposition from militant workers*' to all of the speakers at the May Day celebrations in Liverpool. Clement Attlee was barracked so hard, he had to sit

---

[45] https://en.wikipedia.org/wiki/J._F._C._Fuller
[46] *Liverpool Echo* '*Platform overturned: Court sequel to clash between parties.* 28 Sept 1936
[47] *Liverpool Echo* '*Communists and meeting: Liverpool secretary and his violence warning*' 12 Oct 1937'
[48] *Action* 16 Oct 1937

down [49]. Hostility to the leaderships of workers' organisations led to accusations that the CPGB was splitting the labour movement. Attempts to set up 'alternative leadership' in the unions led to the demise of the Minority Movement in the early years of the decade. Even where some members may have agreed with the stance of the Minority Movement, the tradition of union loyalty was too strong to accommodate the militants. The more apparently left wing the leader, the more the alleged dope pedlar was attacked. The churches came in for special attention in this 'dope peddling' regard.

It came as some surprise then for readers of the *Echo* that a meeting had been held between leading members of the Communist Party in Liverpool and ecclesiastical big hitters in 1934. In an early instance of Christian-Communist dialogue the *Echo* could report that the Bishop and Dean of the Anglican Cathedral had met with six leading local communists to discuss the motivation and world view of the Marxists. Included in the Communist team were Jack Hedley and IP Hughes. The article published in the paper under the heading *'Communists at the cathedral: straight talk'* stated that despite the discussions being 'cleared' by the Party leadership, the team had incurred the displeasure of the Party and had been removed from its speakers lists [50]. It is not clear whether this event was at the heart of a disagreement which resulted in a tiny article appearing in the *Daily Worker* on May 18, 1934, under the heading 'Liverpool Expulsions'. In it the expulsion from the party of IP Hughes was announced, giving as the reason 'political unreliability'. Also expelled was Wilfred Fielding of the Young Communist League.

Whatever the reason for the expulsion, the years 1934 and 1935 saw a considerable thawing of the sectarian CPGB policies in Liverpool. In 1935 there was a meeting in the Central Hall which was called to protest against a 'sedition bill' and also rearmament. On the platform was a Liberal politician, Mrs Corbett Ashby[51],

---

[49] *Daily Worker* '*Attlee shouted down*' 4 May 1932.

[50] *Liverpool Echo* 12 February 1934

[51] https://en.wikipedia.org/wiki/Margery_Corbett_Ashby

Olaf Stapledon the groundbreaking science fiction author, a Communist Party speaker and two reverends, one of whom was in the Labour Party. It would be hard to imagine a Communist Party member addressing such a meeting in the late 1920s.

But as the 1930s wore on the platforms the Communist Party appeared on became broader and broader in make-up. The rise of fascism in the UK was one reason for this. But another was the advance of fascism in Spain. From 1936 on, the city saw increasingly well attended meetings called to publicise the events unfolding there. At one in February 1937, a meeting addressed by university professors, Liberals, Labour Party councillors and communists set up an 'Aid for Spain' committee. In March 1937, 6000 people attended a rally in the stadium to hear speakers outline the events unfolding in Austria following the German annexation of that country. In July 1938, 15,000 people attended a rally for Spain in St Georges Hall. In the same month Bessie Braddock chaired a meeting in Garston with her ex-comrade Leo McGree and newly back from Spain, Councillor JL Jones. This was Jack Jones who went on to lead the TGWU for many years.

CHILDREN OF MIGHTY MEN.—Sixty boys and girls whose fathers are fighting in Spain with the British International Brigade, spent a happy day by the sea at Ainsdale. They were under the care of members of the Merseyside Aid Spain Committee. To add to their enjoyment, S. S. Silverman, M.P., and H. Livermore kindly gave 3d. to each child. Picture shows these Liverpool children about to leave for their day's outing.

Luke Hogan, leader of the Labour Party was previously regarded as the hammer of the left for his role in rooting out communists in Liverpool. But he received numerous warm accolades in the *Daily Worker* for his role in organising for Spain. Co-operating with communists must have come at some cost to the leaders of the 'Catholic clique' in charge of the Labour Party. As well as working with militant atheists they must have felt the burden of the church's ambivalent attitude towards the Franco rebellion, and over the rise of fascism itself. The right-wing press had been full of stories about republican mistreatment of catholic clergy in the country.

An example of the difficulties that Liverpool Labour Catholics faced on the question of Spain was illustrated in an article which appeared in the *Daily Worker* on 25 January 1937. Davie Logan, Labour MP for the Scotland division in the city was excoriated in the paper for a speech he made in Parliament about Spain. Logan *'The little businessman who has made his cuckoo's nest in the Labour Party"* made a speech in which he *'repeated all the stale old 'Daily Mail' lies about murdered priests and nuns'*[52]. One year later, Luke Hogan received a favourable report in the *Daily Worker* for collecting money for the embattled republic.

To illustrate the point that that popular-frontism in the city was not all smiles and handshakes, the *Echo* ran a lengthy debate in its letters page in which the first salvo came from the Anglican archbishop. He announced in the paper that he had resigned from a League of Nations organisation in the city because he felt that its activities were becoming 'too communistic'. It is never entirely clear from the letters what this accusation boiled down to. But it was true that an official of the party was a key officer in the League of Nations organisation. This came as a surprise to other correspondents in the debate who swore that the man in question had always proved a personable and hardworking member of the team. But the bishop was not to be budged. Neither were the National Union of Railwaymen who, at their conference in Southport in July, rejected a motion calling for widespread Popular Frontism in the movement.

By the mid 1930s the Communist Party was often making offers to assist the Labour Party in fighting elections. These offers were most often politely declined. But in 1937 Joe Sayle, the father of Alexei Sayle wrote to the *Daily Worker* to thank the Clubmoor

---

[52] *Daily Worker*, '*A Westminster notebook*' 25 Jan, 1937

CPGB for their assistance in fighting a municipal election campaign [53]. Sayle would later become a well-known Communist Party member in Liverpool.

But as the war in Spain dragged on, pressure to work together with ideological opponents intensified. The *Daily Worker* even carried an article from Liverpool which made positive comments about a city Liberal Party member. In January of 1939 Frank Bright, JL Houston, an ex-party member now standing for the Labour Party and Jimmy Grady, the newly appointed sub district organiser led a march through the city about Spain, even though by this stage they must have seen the writing on the wall for the Spanish government. Jack Coward, an International Brigade volunteer, returned to Liverpool after being feared dead following capture by fascist forces. He wrote a book '*Back from the Dead*' which recounted his experiences which was serialised in the *Daily Worker*. In March, one month before the final surrender of the republican government in April 1939, Aneurin Bevan stood on a platform with Stafford Cripps, himself recently expelled from the Labour Party for his Popular Front advocacy. 4000 people attended a meeting at which the mood must have been hard to elevate. By the end of the war the focus became the care of refugees and the fate of the families of volunteers who never came home.

# Industrial activity of the CPGB in Liverpool

While the party centre could complain with some justice that the membership in Liverpool was skewed towards the unemployed, the truth was that the class which had been previously working was now, in huge numbers, on the dole. Through the NUWM the Communist Party had attempted to organise the unemployed into the many hunger marches of the period and other activities demanding 'work or maintenance'. But for every worker who lost his or her job there was an increased

---

[53] *Daily Worker*, 6 Nov, 1937

difficulty in organising among the remaining workforce. The city had special problems in this regard. The local economy relied on much casual employment: the docks, seafaring and building. These had been hit hard in the depression.

There were some bright notes in the early 1930s though. Charlie Hoyle was well known in the AEU and sat on its district committee. He was also on the district committee of the Engineers' Minority Movement. Leo McGree was on the district committee of the Amalgamated Society of Woodworkers but was out of work so much that he was also the Liverpool secretary of the NUWM. Ex councillor Jack Nield was its chair. But although the Daily Worker reported the enthusiastic adoption of Minority Movement resolutions by dockers in 1931 [54], and the founding of an NUR Minority Movement branch in Birkenhead, the heyday of that organisation was over. For a short time, the Communist Party nationally attempted to breathe new life into the organisation by launching the Workers Charter, based on the People's charter movement of the 1840s. But it was too late for the Minority Movement and in a short time it was wound up.

However, there was still life in the trade union movement, and it could still flex its muscles. But this was not always to the Communist Party's advantage. Charlie Heaton from the Clubmoor local was expelled from the Trade's Council in 1932[55] because of his membership of the Communist Party. In 1934 Charlie Hoyle had his election materials for the post of AEU president 'censored', by the union returning officer. He had described the agreement drawn up between the AEU and the employers as being based on 'a lying argument'. 'Liverpool Engineer' (possibly Hoyle himself) described in an article in the *Daily Worker* how this unprecedented interference in an election had come about [56].

---

[54] *Daily Worker* '*Dockers turn down bureaucrats*' 23 May, 1931
[55] *Daily Worker* 22 Dec, 1932
[56] Liverpool Engineer '*Engineers secretary censors militant's election address*' *Daily Worker* 23 Aug, 1934

But apart from some skirmishes the industrial scene for the Liverpool party was rather quiet in the mid 1930s. In 1935 there was another attempt to breathe life into rank and file activism with the organisation in the city of a branch of a new shop stewards movement[57]. One notable feature of the meeting was its delegate list. At its inaugural meeting in the TGWU headquarters, addressed by Tom Mann, the Electrical Trade Union (ETU) was represented by an up-and-coming militant called Frank Foulkes. Foulkes would go on to become embroiled in the ETU vote rigging scandal of 1961. When the vote rigging was exposed in a famous trial it brought a ferociously anti-communist leadership to the union for a generation. The damage caused to the Communist Party's reputation for honesty was almost irretrievably lost.

Foulkes next appeared in the news at the heart of a large strike which broke out in an aircraft factory in Speke. In June 1939, 6000 men came out on strike to demand the reinstatement of an AEU steward who had been sacked [58]. Foulkes, though he represented electricians, addressed the workers outside the factory, which made aeroplanes for the coming conflict. This would not be the last time that the tension between war work and industrial action would be felt by the Communist Party.

# Cultural Marxism: The cultural life of the Liverpool CPGB

In many ways the cultural life of Communist Party members in the 1930s resembled that of other fields of communist life at the time: cramped by sectarian constraints. Insofar as these activities were written about or advertised in the *Daily Worker* , they were somewhat limited in the period 1930 - 1934. But in the middle of

---

[57] *Daily Worker, 'Liverpool meet which heralds shop stewards revival'* 10 Aug, 1935
[58] *Daily Worker 'They sacked steward so 6000 men stopped work'* 15 June, 1939.

the decade there was a flowering of cultural activities. Their number and nature brings a phrase to mind which Manuilsky of the Comintern used to describe the CPGB. Meant as a serious criticism of British communism and to berate the British comrades' lack of seriousness and want of professionalism, he called the CPGB 'a society of great friends'.

In the early thirties the advertised cultural offer of the party could be divided between cinema and theatre. There were exceptions to this scheme. One or two adverts indicate that an Esperanto group was active in the Liverpool party. For several years in the early 30s the party ran a 'Lenin - Liebknecht week' which included cultural as well as political events [59]. In 1930 there was a worker's theatre group. There was also a branch of the Workers Film Society offering films, usually but not exclusively sourced from the USSR. For instance, they had a showing of the German film 'The Cabinet of Dr Caligari'[60] But mostly the films were uplifting Soviet titles intended to carry a political message. Even the Workers Theatre Group followed this model. In January 1930 they carried two plays described by the *Daily Worker* as 'translations from the Russian'. Their titles carry with them the flavour of the times. One was called 'The Traitor' and one was called 'The New Saint'. Interest in the new cinema extended beyond the ranks of the party. There was some controversy in the pages of the *Liverpool Echo* when it was alleged that the programme of the Liverpool Film Society was dedicated to the promotion of Soviet films and by extension, of communism. This allegation was roundly denied by the society's management committee [61]. In one of its 1931 meetings the Workers Film Society had Ralph Bond to speak on the subject of 'The theory and practice of workers cinema'. As well as being the leader of the Left-Wing Movement, Bond became himself a noted documentary

---

[59] *Daily Worker*, '*Lenin- Liebknecht week: Liverpool efforts for united front against war*' 6 Jan 1931
[60] https://en.wikipedia.org/wiki/The_Cabinet_of_Dr._Caligari
[61] *Liverpool Echo*, *The film society and propaganda*. 9 May, 1930.

maker focussing on the lives of ordinary people faced with demanding events [62].

In the background throughout this period the Liverpool branch of the Friends of the Soviet Union also showed Soviet films with more or less success. But little more in the way of cultural life was advertised until December of 1933, when the London Red Players put on a 'two hour show' in support of International Labour Defence in Birkenhead and Liverpool. The practice of showing Soviet films was not by any means exclusively restricted to the early 1930s. An advert from the Communist Party in the *Liverpool Echo* of 24 Nov 1939 offered a Ukrainian film entitled 'The Rich Bride', but the suspicion must be entertained that the real motive of the meeting was to hear Frank Bright, by now the Lancashire organiser of the party, speak on the subject of 'The workers and the war'.

It was not until the period of the Popular Front that cultural matters in the Communist Party began to warm up. In January of 1937 there was the first advert for the Left Book Club. In September of that year the Merseyside Left Book Club Theatre Guild were billed to play at the Unity Theatre Club at Kings Cross in London to perform 'Before Guernica' and 'Insurgents Aid Committee' by Edgar Criddle. Along with Gerry Dawson, Criddle founded the theatre company which went on to become Liverpool Unity Theatre in Hope Place [63]. In January of 1938 the Garston branch of the Left Book Club was addressed by the noted novelist and political commentator Arthur Koestler who came to speak about his recently published memoir of the war in Spain '*Spanish Testament*' in which he recounted his experiences working behind the fascist lines at the heart of Francos war machine. He maintained his cover by using his credentials as a *News Chronicle* journalist. Later on, Koestler would write the profoundly anti

---

62

http://www.screenonline.org.uk/people/id/554490/index.html
[63] https://matthewlinley.wordpress.com/2014/11/20/new-beginnings-and-a-move-from-east-to-west/

Leninist book '*Darkness at Noon*' [64]. In June 1939 Olaf Stapeldon, the Wirral based science fiction author and philosopher, addressed a meeting of the Left Book Club at 62 Hope Street on 'The new propaganda'. His novel Starmaker has been credited as being one of the most influential science fiction works ever. It was said to be the inspiration for Arthur C Clarke's '2001' [65]

In 1937 the Communist Party produced a 'Pageant of Labour History' in Shiel Park. 800 people showed up to see floats and presentations depicting scenes from Labour history. Following the pageant, a rally was held in a local cinema [66]. In September of 1938 the Communist Party held a similar event which the *Daily Worker* claimed was attended by 10,000 [67]. Pageants of this nature were common on the left of the 1930s, but Liverpool's pageant was considered a notable success [68]. In the same month as the pageant there was a melancholy event to celebrate the names of the men who had died fighting fascism in Spain. It was organised by the Wounded and Dependents Aid Committee. This was a broad organisation but was clearly supported by the local Communist Party. It featured Paul Robeson who gave his services free to the fund-raising event [69].

A feature of the cultural life of the Communist Party in the late 1930s was the increasing number of social events which were held. Barely a month went by in the late 1930s without some sort of party being advertised. The early 1930s had very few. One was advertised in 1933 and was described as a 'Smoking concert' and

[64] https://en.wikipedia.org/wiki/Arthur_Koestler

[65] https://en.wikipedia.org/wiki/Olaf_Stapledon

[66] Daily Worker, '*Historic pageant at Liverpool*' 21 Sept 1937

[67] Daily Worker '*Men of north march with Tom Mann*' 27 Sept 1938

[68] Wallis, M. *Pageantry and the Popular Front: Ideological Production in the 'Thirties*. New Theatre Quarterly, 1994 *10*(38), 132-156.

[69] Daily Worker '*Liverpool honours heroes*' 22 Sept 1938

was held in the Washington hotel, opposite Lime Street station. Perhaps this was in response to the jibe of the party investigatory committee that poor recruitment was due to poor social activity. By the end of the 1930s socials were being held at 8 Lilley Road in Fairfield on an almost monthly basis. According to Kelly's street index, this address was occupied by a Mrs Elizabeth Foulkes. The similarity with the name of Frank Foulkes cannot be ignored. This address was also given as the site of numerous meetings and events in the period.

## The life and soul of the Party

Life for a communist in the city was very busy throughout the 1930s. New organisations, committees and campaigns were frequently featured in the *Daily Worker* . Aside from the party local meetings and the trade union branches, each with their own spin off sub committees and higher, district and national bodies there were the campaigns that all party members would have been expected to participate in. Many of these organisations will have been proscribed from the Labour Party, precisely because so many communists turned up at meetings. There was the Minority Movement, the International Labour Defence, The Workers Charter groups, the NUWM, peace campaigns, the Friends of the Soviet Union, the League Against Imperialism and the Workers Film Society. Then there were the committees designed to help with the hunger marches. And this was all before the conflicts with fascism and the war in Spain began and created their own cascades of new groups to populate. Added to these activities the Left Book Club must take some prominence.

As early as 1930 the *Daily Worker* publicised news stories about the racial politics of Liverpool and on June 23 the paper reported that an International Seamen's club had been formed in the Wapping area of the docks. The article is specific about the intention of the club to divert 'colonial' seafarers away from the traditional venues used in the city *'that are the curse of all seafarers and the willing institutions of the National Union of*

*Seamen*[70] By August in 1930 the *Daily Worker* could report a large rally for 'negro seamen' and the formation of an organisation which demanded equal pay for 'colonial' sailors. This organisation had strong links with the Minority Movement and was very hostile to the leadership of the NUS which was described in the article as 'Fascist' [71]. The party in the city also gave considerable publicity to the case of the 'Scottsboro boys' culminating in the Liverpool party organising a meeting on June 17 to hear one of the mothers of the accused who had come to the UK to speak about the affair. The case involved nine black teenagers who were accused of raping two white women, and subsequently faced the death penalty. There was an international outcry against the treatment of the boys by the courts in Alabama.[72]

As well as the meetings designed to address specific issues the party offered meetings of a philosophical nature. In 1930 Charlie Hoyle and Leo McGree addressed a meeting on the subject of communism and religion. In 1937 William Rust was advertised in the *Liverpool Echo* for a lecture on 'Communism', while in the same month CPGB philosopher Maurice Dobb was advertised offering a lecture on 'Materialism' in the city.

---

[70] *Daily Worker* 'Boon to all seamen: International club opens in Liverpool' 23 June 1930
[71] *Daily Worker* ' Negro seamen rally in Liverpool: Organisation to fight wage cut threats' 5 August 1930
[72] https://en.wikipedia.org/wiki/Scottsboro_Boys

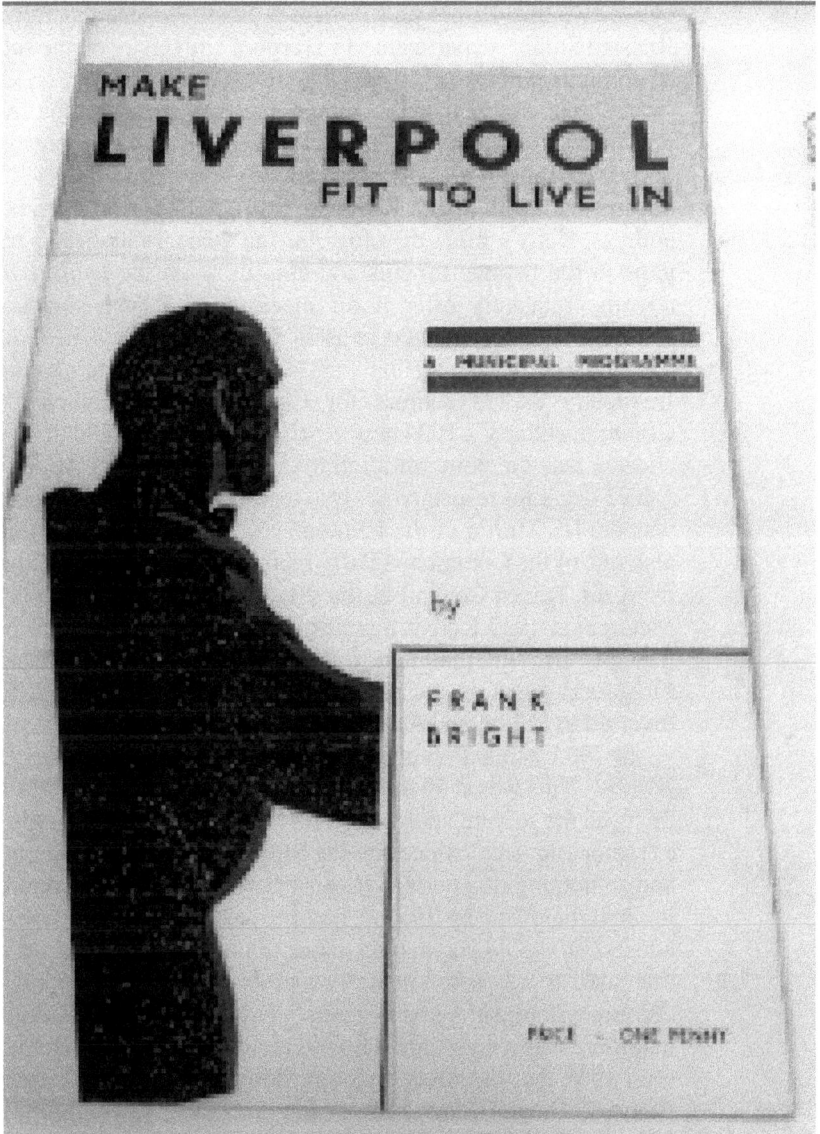

MAKE
**LIVERPOOL**
FIT TO LIVE IN

A MUNICIPAL PROGRAMME

by

FRANK
BRIGHT

PRICE — ONE PENNY

In September of 1937 the *Echo* reported that the Larkhill
Debating Society on Muirhead Avenue were hosting a debate

between Frank Bright and Professor Basil Slepchenko from the Russian Studies department of Liverpool University on the subject of communism.

As well as organising meetings the party struggled to create a presence for its literature. The first address given for people to pick up party publications was Marmaduke Street. But after 1930 this became 36 Smith Street, Kirkdale. It is not clear who lived in this address. Kelly's street directory for the years 1930 - 1933 reveal gaps in the listings for this address, although the *Daily Worker* adverts frequently offer it for meetings and even socials. A different address emerged in 1934 for a 'Party Day' in January. The address for the meeting was 38 Edge Lane and this became a frequently quoted address for Communist Party events. The Communist Party's 1934 new year's eve party was held there. The address was the home of a tailor and a joiner, Harry Martin and John Fitzgerald respectively. It is tempting to think that the tailor was the HS Martin of the Islington riot trial of 1932. Martin was also one of the Communist Party members who had been expelled from the Trades Council in the 20s with Charlie Hoyle and Leo McGree. In 1937 Kelly's directory described the address as being that of the 'International Labour Defence Club' with John Fitzgerald given as the name of the secretary. By 1939 it had reverted to Martin and Fitzgerald once more.

In 1933 another source of literature was quoted in the *Daily Worker*. This was at 50 Ashfield in Wavertree. From 1933 to 1939 this was the private address of one William Ebbage, described as a 'motor engineer'. Since leaving Marmaduke Street the party had had something of a peripatetic history, with no obvious centre for its activities. But by 1939 it had moved into a more permanent address at 19 Old Haymarket, close to the Mersey tunnel. In 1937 this address was listed in Kelly's street directory as the home of 'Workers Publications, publishers.' This name gives a strong hint that there was a communist link to its tenants in 1937. But it isn't until 1939 that the street directory describes it as the Communist Party of Great Britain Merseyside Sub District Committee. In 1938 Frank Bright published a 'programme for Liverpool' called *'Make Liverpool a fit place to live in'*.

As well as attending the myriad meetings associated with the party's many activities there was the constant requirement to maintain the sales of the *Daily Worker* . We have seen already that the Communist Party in Liverpool was subject to frequent and severe reprimand in the pages of the paper for their underperformance in this field. In order to achieve an eight-page version of the paper Liverpool would have to sell 150 'quire' of papers to meet its allocated target [73]. A quire of papers was 24. Criticism of this nature seemed to tail off in the middle of the decade and by the end of the 1930 *Daily Worker* activity expanded out into new and unfamiliar fields. The Communist Party established something called the *Daily Worker League* and allied to that, *Daily Worker* reading groups. It is not clear how many of these readers groups came into existence. But the *Daily Worker League* seemed to concentrate on social events as much as political ones. Days out to the Wirral were advertised as well as rambling trips. One of the League groups had the *Daily Worker* journalist Frank Pitcairn to speak. This was the *Daily Worker* nom de plume of the celebrated journalist Claud Cockburn. In 1939 the League was due to hold a spectacular gala day, involving sports and social events. Unable to entirely lay down the political nature of the event it was due to be addressed by William Gallacher MP. That it was held on the Rathbone fields off Greenbank Road, courtesy of the Rathbone family, demonstrated just how far Popular Frontism had succeeded in taking the Communist Party into political acceptance. In the end torrential rain ruined the event.

# Darkening clouds: International activity

From its inception in 1920 the CPGB had a constant eye on various aspects of the 'international situation'. In part this was due to the level of priority given to the defence of the USSR from counter revolutionary and western interventions. But there were other themes at play, some of which had special significance for

---

[73] *Daily Worker 'Liverpool Out For Big Job'* 17 Oct 1935

Liverpool as a major port. Take for instance the activity in the port to defend China from the attentions of Imperial Japan. Echoing the 'Hands Off Russia' campaign in London at the time of the Russian revolution, Liverpool had its own 'Hands Off China' meetings in February 1932, with a demonstration calling for peace in China in March of that year. In addition, anti-Japanese resolutions were passed at the May Day march in 1932. The events in China may have been overshadowed by other international events closer to home during the 1930s but they never entirely went away. In 1937 for instance some 2000 people assembled outside the Japanese consulate in the city to protest about the bombing of Canton and to call for local dockers to refuse to load or unload Japanese boats. When a delegation went in to deliver the protest the Consul became enraged when the deputation refused to shake his hand [74].

But in European terms, a priority of the party's international work in the 1930s was in the promotion of the USSR and in the international fight against fascism. There were some other lines of activity. There were large meetings about Ireland in the city organised by the district. In 1932 there was a large meeting organised by the League Against Imperialism addressed by Sean Murray [75]. These became more relevant in 1939 when an IRA bombing campaign started in Britain, targeting sites in Liverpool. This included an attack on the tram lines on Aigburth Road close to the cricket ground. The police discovered a lock up garage packed with explosives in Lilley Road, Fairfield just yards away from the home of the East Liverpool Communist Party branch at 8 Lilley Road. There were also meetings held to understand the developing situation in Palestine, with Ben Bradley[76] delivering talks at the Liverpool East branch and in Birkenhead. A series of Communist Party meetings were held throughout Merseyside in

[74] *Daily Worker 'Liverpool calls for embargo'* 1 Oct 1937
[75] https://www.jstor.org/stable/24897203
[76]

https://www.open.ac.uk/researchprojects/makingbritain/content/ben-bradley

1938 about the collapse of the democracies in the defence of Czechoslovakia.

When Charlie Hoyle returned from his two years study in Russia at the International Lenin School his services were widely touted by the Party and also by the Friends of the Soviet Union. In the Birkenhead branch Hoyle debated with Professor Basil

---

★ **In the BIRKENHEAD District** ★

A DEBATE, at "BEECHCROFT," WHET-STONE LANE, BIRKENHEAD, Wednesday, April 26, 7.45 p.m., "That Five-Year Plan and Proletarian Dictatorship Are a Success. CHARLIE HOYLE, for F.S.U., v. B. SLEPCHENKO. Seats, 6d., 3d., and limited number free.

## INTERNATIONAL LABOUR DEFENCE
### (BIRKENHEAD SECTION)
## GRAND CINEMA PERFORMANCE

of SOVIET FILMS, Scientific, Cultural, Educational, "THE GENERAL LINE" and "THE ROOF OF THE WORLD," will be held in

## "BEECHCROFT," WHETSTONE LANE

Monday and Tuesday, May 1 and 2.
Doors open 7.0 p.m. Commence 7.30 p.m.

Admission by programme only. 1s., obtainable at 21 IVY STREET and 8, COLE STREET, BIRKENHEAD; 8, FLORENCE ROAD, SEACOMBE; 13, WOODWARD ROAD, ROCK FERRY. 27, BEACONSFIELD ROAD, TRANMERE.

---

Schlepchenko of Liverpool University on the subject of the USSRs five-year plan in 1933.

There was a second Russia related series of meetings organised by the FSU. These concerned the so-called Metro Vick trial. In its haste to electrify the Soviet Union and in the face of the shortage of qualified engineers to build the necessary infrastructure, the Soviet authorities contracted in foreign specialists to complete the work. Among these foreign specialists were electrical engineers from the Metro Vickers works in Manchester. They were employed in Moscow in 1932. These were dangerous times for technicians in the USSR. The trial of 'the Industrial Party' specialists in Moscow [77] had signalled the start of a wave of official paranoia about the alleged wrecking activities of people at the heart of Soviet industry. In January 1933 Stalin himself accused unnamed persons as wishing to open a frontal assault on Soviet power: '*Hence, the only thing left for them is to do mischief and harm to the workers, to the collective farmers, to the Soviet regime, and to the Party. And they are doing as much mischief as they can, acting on the sly. They set fire to warehouses and wreck machinery. They organise sabotage*'. It was into this climate that the Manchester engineers went about their work. On January 25, 1933, the head of the Metro Vickers mission was taken to the Lubyanka prison and interrogated. Six of his colleagues were subsequently arrested and put on trial. Two were sent to prison for 2 and 3 years and the rest were expelled. In June 1933 an engineer and AEU member who had worked in Moscow on the Metro Vickers scheme, referred to as 'Comrade Beaumont' in the *Daily Worker* advert, came over to Liverpool to speak about the trial. It is not recorded whether his version of events supported the case of his AEU colleagues or that of the NKVD.

But the focus of much of the Communist Party's international work in Liverpool was in the fight against fascism. This started early with a mass meeting in Birkenhead to protest about the Reichstag fire trial in 1933. On October 6, 1935, Tom Mann addressed a crowd claimed to be 1200 protesting against the Italian fascist's attack on Abyssinia. But when the war in Spain started the activities of the party in fighting international fascism became

---

[77] https://en.wikipedia.org/wiki/Industrial_Party_Trial

an almost nightly event. No platform was too broad, no committee was too specialised for communists to participate in. The strictures of the third period were, for the moment, entirely abandoned. The *Daily Worker* reported meetings in the city collecting milk for Spain, food ships were filled with supplies and refugees catered for. The *Daily Worker* also exposed the address of the Falange party in 'Sefton Park Drive'. It is not clear whether the typesetter at the *Daily Worker* meant Sefton Park Road or Sefton Drive in their report. This wasn't the only occasion when foreign fascist meetings were held in the city, sometimes under the cover of diplomatic activity. On July 17, 1939, the *Daily Worker* reported a meeting of the Nazi Labour Front for Northern England which was held in the German consulate in Rodney Street [78]. The door was guarded by men in dark in uniforms. The article describing these events itself demonstrated how far in the city Popular Frontism had gone. It approvingly cited the activity of a local politician who attempted unsuccessfully to enter the meeting. An opponent of Nazi propaganda in the city, he was refused entry by the blackshirted doormen and was thrown out. He was Mr Stinton Johnson, a local Tory agent. This was not the only occasion that the Rodney Street address had been the cover for undiplomatic activities. The consul had been asked to leave Britain because of his role in an espionage scandal [79]. This led to a 'diplomatic incident' involving tit for tat expulsions of British officials from Germany.

One of the oddest international episodes of the period concerned the fate of International Brigade volunteer Frank Ryan. On 27 June 1939 the *Daily Worker* reported a meeting that had taken place in Wigan. At this meeting Birkenhead communist leader Joe Rawlings made the case for the release of Frank Ryan

---

[78] *Daily Worker* '*20 Nazi agents in Liverpool meeting*' 17 June, 1939
[79] https://bygoneliverpool.wordpress.com/2020/12/06/a-nazi-consulate-in-rodney-street/

from a Francoist prison [80]. Ryan was an Irish republican and member of the Connolly column of Irish Marxist volunteers. He had been the editor of the leftist Republican Congress paper An Phoblacht in the 1930s. In Spain he was captured by the Italians and imprisoned in Burgos. While there he was visited by an Irish consul who secured his release, but it was straight into the hands of the German army. Ryan voluntarily accompanied them to Berlin where he stayed until his death in 1944, acting as an Abwehr - IRA liaison officer planning joint operations against the British [81]. Unaware of these developments, British communists kept up a 'Free Frank Ryan' campaign into the 1940s.

# Liverpool communists and peace campaigns in the 1930s

On reading the efforts of Liverpool communists throughout the 1930s one is struck by how much of that effort was devoted to campaigning for peace. Anti-war activities were widespread and plentiful throughout Merseyside in this period. This activity did not spring from any pacifist sentimentality, although many of the Communist Party's activists had been conscientious objectors in WW1 and, as in the case of IP Hughes, had paid the price in prison years. Indeed the columns of the *Daily Worker* frequently hosted authors fiercely critical of pacifism. It was rather that communists thought that without constant opposition the power of the capitalist west would be unleashed against the USSR. This belief was not without some foundation. The western interventions in support of counter revolution in 1917 was still fresh in the minds of communists. The talk of rearmament in the 30s only fuelled these suspicions. But the rise of Nazism in Germany, and the invasions of China by Japan which took hostile troops right up to the Soviet border gave these theoretical threats new, practical reality. Anti-

---

[80] *Daily Worker 'Meeting calls for Ryans release'* 27 June 1939
[81]

https://en.wikipedia.org/wiki/Frank_Ryan_(Irish_republican)

war sentiment in the CPGB had two main components, although there were subsidiary aims, as we shall see. The first was to oppose anything resembling the imperialist war of 1914 when the tectonic plates of conflicting empires collided and took the lives of millions of workers in the ensuing chaos. The second was to defend at all costs the existence of the first socialist state and to oppose military aggression against the USSR as a top priority.

The first reports in the *Daily Worker* of peace work were in 1934 when an advert placed by the League Against Imperialism announced that a conference was to take place to establish a Merseyside Peace Committee. The rest of 1934 was taken up with campaigning against a bill which was designed to punish those (such as numerous communists, including the local activist Nugent Coffey) who directed pleas to soldiers not to fire upon workers when called to during strikes, colonial unrest or in Ireland. A Merseyside Anti Sedition Bill Committee was set up which organised large gatherings in Picton Hall and the Liverpool stadium. The meeting involved novelist Olaf Stapledon, Sydney Silverman, the radical local lawyer and, latterly, member of parliament and JBS Haldane, the populariser of modern science. In June 1935 ex MP Shapurji Saklatvala shared a platform with Leo McGree to publicise 'The Communist Party and the fight against war'. But it was not only in campaigning against war that the Communist Party got involved. It also supported efforts to protect the population from war should it happen. Favourable reports appeared in the *Daily Worker* about campaigns in Liverpool such as the Merseyside Armaments Protest Committee who, in August 1935, insisted upon adequate gas mask provision and practical blackout training.

After the start of the Spanish civil war any idea that the Communist Party was pursuing a pacifist policy was finally killed off. Not only did the Communist Party favour the arming of the Spanish government they favoured active diplomatic and even military support for the republic. The Communist Party on Merseyside supported these claims with boots on the ground. The party was in the forefront of organising the illegal transport of

volunteers to fight against fascism on the Spanish peninsula, and many of the young men who went did not come home. Numerous members of the local Communist Party leadership who had appeared in the city's courts went to fight: Jack Hedley, Charlie Martinson, Albert Cole, Owen Kelly and Frank Deegan to name a few. By 1938 the propaganda from the party relating to the oncoming conflict became more focussed. In May of that year a meeting in Birkenhead asked the question 'Would a peace alliance work?'. The Peace Alliance was an initiative supported by the Communist Party which proposed an alliance of forces opposed to fascism and war, composed of the broadest set of domestic forces yet conceived. This is what the Birkenhead meeting was designed to advocate. Liverpool North branch of the Communist Party followed this up with a meeting of their own, addressed by ex-Communist Party man, now a Labour candidate in the local elections, Jack Houston. In September Pollitt amplified this message at a rally in Liverpool calling for 'collective security' against fascist aggression.

In February 1939 the *Echo* reported a debate which had taken place in Bebington involving communists about the degree of preparation that the country had made for air raid precautions. In the same month Leo McGree, Frank Bright and the newly appointed Liverpool organiser Jim Grady addressed a 'Crusade for the defence of the people' meeting at the Picton Hall. In April of that year the Spanish civil war ended with the defeat of the republican government and the scattering of refugees throughout Europe. This must have left large gaps in the calendars of many people on the left. The meetings, the committees, the collections and the marches of the previous years must have come to a sharp, if foreseen stop.

But while anti-fascists were digesting the implications of the defeat in Spain, fascist wheels were still turning. Japan was wreaking havoc in the far east and Nazi outrages were occurring in Czechoslovakia and Austria. The Kindertransport escape trains were bringing children out of Nazi countries to Britain. Many of the children ended up in a hostel on Linnet Lane in Liverpool. Then, like a bolt from the blue, Bright, Pollitt and Grady had to hold meetings to explain more awkward developments. In August of 1939 it was announced that the USSR and Nazi Germany had come to an arrangement where they undertook not to engage in aggression towards each other for at least a decade. Further shocks were to come in September for party members who had cut their teeth on the anti-fascist struggle. In that month Germany attacked Poland. For prime minister Chamberlain this meant that all of his efforts to appease Hitler had come to nothing and war was declared. But to the dismay of many communists, the leadership of the party decided that, given that the USSR was 'at peace' with Nazi Germany, there was nothing for workers to fight for in any imminent war. Although Harry Pollitt and a rear-guard of communists in the leadership of the Communist Party supported the war, the majority on the central committee followed the Comintern and opposed it. From November to December the party in Liverpool ran meeting after meeting to explain this change of approach to the struggle against fascism and for many it was an incomprehensible change of tack. In the Working-Class Movement Library in Manchester there is a cassette tape made by Eddie Frow, the founder of the library. It is of a meeting held in Liverpool in the 1980s which reviewed the life of the party in Liverpool in the twenties and thirties. An unidentified speaker is recorded giving his memories of the disputes which took place in the city at the decision to oppose the war. He said that he and a Young Communist League friend went to a 'very well attended meeting' of the Liverpool South branch of the party in Garston. He said that virtually the entire packed house spoke in favour of the line of Harry Pollitt in supporting the war effort. He also commented wryly that as well as being the only two to oppose the war and support the leadership, he and his friend were the only two young enough to be conscripted.

At the end of 1939 then, it appeared that the political capital assiduously accumulated by the Communist Party through the hard years of the 1930s was about to be squandered. The party may well have said on its application form, printed in the *Daily Worker* in October 1939 that *'This war is a fight between imperialist powers over profits, colonies and world domination. All warring parties are equally responsible'* but it must have been a difficult line to maintain when the children were being packed off to evacuation and the bombs started to fall on the port. To followers of Pollitt's minority pro-war opinion it must have seemed as though once again the party was entering a period of sectarian self-isolation. And once again this isolation was due to its slavish pursuit of loyalty to the Communist Party of the Soviet Union, whose political priorities were at odds with the commitments made by the British party. At that low point in the development of the party there can have been few in the CPGB who could foresee that the coming decade would see the party enter the golden years of its recruitment and influence.

# Biographical notes

## Bamber, Mary  1874 - 1938

Mrs Mary Bamber had been born into a wealthy family in a rich part of Edinburgh. But her father turned to drink and left the family, and this drove his wife and children into poverty. They followed the son of the family to Liverpool where young Mary

Bamber became more and more involved in the trade union and political struggles in the city. She became a Labour councillor in Everton, a part of the city riven by sectarian hostilities. Before the first world war she was active with other socialists in providing soup to the unemployed from a van supplied by the socialist newspaper *The Clarion*

# Biographical notes

## Bamber, Mary 1874 - 1938

Mrs Mary Bamber had been born into a wealthy family in a rich part of Edinburgh. But her father turned to drink and left the family, and this drove his wife and children into poverty. They followed the son of the family to Liverpool where young Mary Bamber became more and more involved in the trade union and political struggles in the city. She became a Labour councillor in Everton, a part of the city riven by sectarian hostilities. Before the first world war she was active with other socialists in providing soup to the unemployed from a van supplied by the socialist newspaper *The Clarion*

CITY OF LIVERPOOL.

EVERTON WARD.

MUNICIPAL BYE-ELECTION.

WEDNESDAY, 7th MAY, 1902

NO NONSENSE this time.

VOTE STRAIGHT for the LABOUR CANDIDATE

VOTERS of EVERTON YOU now have a Real Opportunity to have as YOUR Civic Representative a True Industrial Candidate.

With the Compliments of

Mrs. MARY BAMBER, LABOUR CANDIDATE.

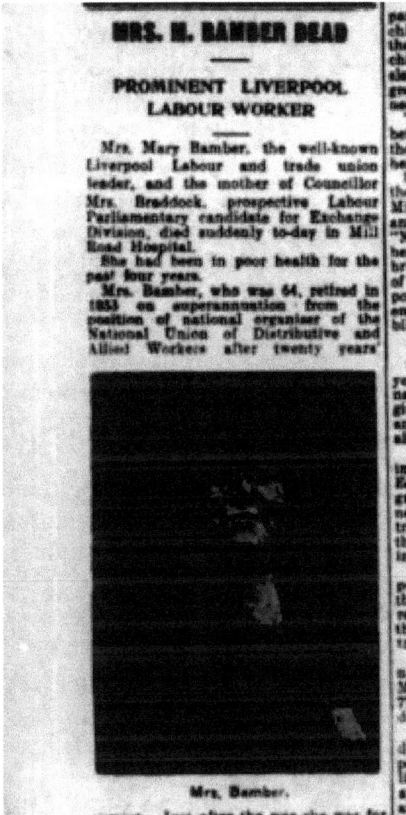

MRS. M. BAMBER DEAD

PROMINENT LIVERPOOL
LABOUR WORKER

Mrs. Mary Bamber, the well-known Liverpool Labour and trade union leader, and the mother of Councillor Mrs. Braddock, prospective Labour Parliamentary candidate for Exchange Division, died suddenly to-day in Mill Road Hospital.

She had been in poor health for the past four years.

Mrs. Bamber, who was 64, retired in 1933 on superannuation from the position of national organiser of the National Union of Distributive and Allied Workers after twenty years

Mrs. Bamber.

She was described by Sylvia Pankhurst as: 'the finest fighting platform speaker in the country'[82], and she spoke at events organised by the Women's Social and Political Union. Mary Bamber was a tireless union activist recruiting women in the poorest paid industrial sectors. She was a stalwart of the East Liverpool branch of the British Socialist Party. She became a foundation member of the Communist Party and was a delegate to its foundation conference. She went as a delegate to the second 1920 congress of the Third International in Moscow.

She was one of the defendants in the 'Art gallery' trial of 1921. The distraction from her union activities was given as the reason why, in 1924, she left the CPGB. Despite this, she remained popular with Communist Party members and a glowing obituary

[82] Pat Ayers 'Free Radical' Nerve 9, Autumn 2006
https://web.archive.org/web/20070224090102/http://www.cat
alystmedia.org.uk/issues/nerve9/bamber_mary.php

appeared in the *Daily Worker* on the occasion of her death in 1938.

## Bright, Frank
## 1891 - 1944

Edmund and Ruth Frow wrote an undated biographical pamphlet about Frank Bright which was published by the North West History Group of the Communist Party [83]

Frank Bright was born in Bideford in Devon on 20th February 1891. He came from a working-class background: his father was a wrought iron worker and his mother looked after Bright and his five siblings. Looking for work he moved to the village of Ynyshir in South Wales to take up work as a miner. Migration from the south west of England to the mining areas of Wales was common before the first world war. The miner's leader AJ Cook had followed a similar path. In the village there was already a group of Marxist miners which included Arthur Horner, one of the most famous communists of his generation.

In 1920 Bright became a founding member of the Communist Party. He was also very active in the miners Minority Movement. During the General Strike in South Wales he helped publish a duplicated paper for the local mines on behalf of the Communist Party called the New Star. This caused him to be arrested for the possession of 'seditious literature'. He was jailed for two months.

---

[83] Frow E, Frow R, *'Frank Bright: Miner, Marxist and Communist 1891- 1944'* North West History Group of the Communist Party

In 1927 Bright moved to Manchester where he took up the post of organiser for the Manchester district. In August 1930 he went to the International Lenin School in Moscow. While there Bright worked in Soviet mines offering advice on technical matters. Conditions in the pits were primitive and during one spell at work Bright contracted pneumonia and required hospital admission. His chest never fully recovered from this episode. His efforts in the mines were recognised by his election to the Moscow Soviet. His fluency in Russian enabled him to become a lecturer in the school. In 1932 Bright spent some time working in Berlin and fell foul of the authorities which resulted in another prison sentence.

In 1935 he became the Liverpool sub district organiser. He was active in the organisation of dock workers, assisting in numerous rank and file publications aimed at improving the conditions of work there. In 1937 he published the pamphlet '*Make Liverpool Fit to Live In*'. Ten thousand of them were published and four thousand of these were purchased by three Liverpool Labour Party organisations.

Bright returned to his previous post as Lancashire organiser but after a couple of months returned to his role in Liverpool. An enthusiastic opponent of the war in 1939 he delivered numerous meetings which pressed the claim that the war was one of imperial rivalries, the official line that the Party took.

By 1942 his health had deteriorated to the point that he returned to Bideford, although he remained very active, becoming the Devon and Cornwall organiser.

He died in 1944 after a long and painful illness. In addition to his funeral in Devon, a memorial service was held for him in Manchester, led by Harry Pollitt.

### Coward, Jack 16 Scargreen Avenue aged 31 in 1936.

*Main source:*
*https://grahamstevenson.me.uk/2009/10/12/coward-jack/*

An International Brigader who became famous in the 1966 seamen's strike, Jack Coward was born in the Lake District in 1905. At the age of 9 his family moved to look for work to Liverpool, settling in the Brownlow Hill area. There, Jack went to

Pleasant Street school and, as soon as he was able, to become a merchant seafarer.

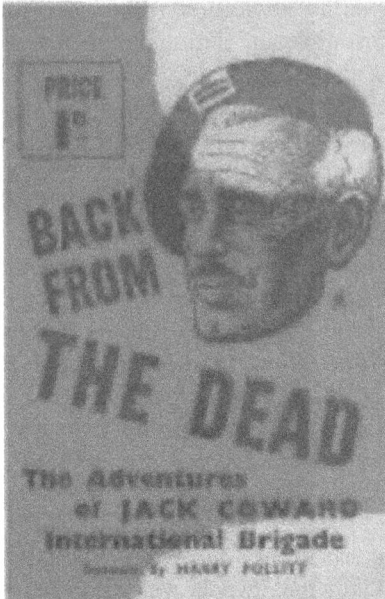

All his life, he was an active trade unionist and life-long member of the Communist Party. Like many of his generation, he was active in the National Unemployed Workers Movement and in street battles with the British Union of Fascists. He was also involved in smuggling fleeing anti-Nazis into Britain.

In November 1936, he left for Spain to assist in the civil war, joining the republican navy in Cartagena. He was later sent to officer training school and on graduation, he was sent to join the No.4 Company of the British Battalion. Coward was captured and imprisoned by the Franco forces for a period. During this time, he was listed as 'missing, presumed dead'. This accounts for the title of his book. On his return home, Jack wrote his 'Back from the Dead', about his time in Spain and published in 1939 by the *Daily Worker* under the Workers Press imprint.

He remained active in the National Union of Seaman, becoming a significant rank and file leader in Liverpool and beyond in the post-war period. Jack Coward also stood as a candidate for the Communist Party in Liverpool local elections.

He was the author of the 1966 Communist Party pamphlet 'We want 40 – the case for the seamen', and the Chair of the London strike committee in the 1966 dispute, becoming named by Harold

Wilson as one of the 'tightly-knit group of politically motivated men'.

## Cole, Albert Edward  of Copeland Street, Everton. 30 in 1932.

On Feb 4, 1932, the *Liverpool Echo* reported that Albert Cole, an 'alleged communist' had appeared in court charged with stealing a man's bag. The story involved a man called Chapman who was at Central Station and was preparing to go to Manchester to join his ship where he worked as a seaman. Albert Cole was there with two men. Cole was alleged to have approached Chapman saying 'I am on strike. You will not be allowed to go to join your ship'. He took the man's bag and handed it to his alleged accomplices. In court Cole replied to the charge saying 'I am not guilty. I did not take the bag'. Nevertheless, he was placed on remand for a week.

Albert Cole had had an interesting life up to this point. He had been a seaman and a member of the IWW (Wobblies). In the memorial edition of Jack Coward's book 'Back from the Dead' he is described as 'a ringleader of a naval strike which became known as the Invergordon Mutiny'. This claim about an 'Albert Cole' from Coward's book is repeated in a footnote of an American text about the British volunteers in the International Brigade [84]. But this claim does not sit easily with other accounts of Cole's life. Tony Lane said this of Cole: "ex-Wobbly, one of the leading members of the Red International breakaway from the National Amalgamated Society of Sailors and Firemen in Liverpool in 1929 was Albert Cole, ex-seaman, ex-Wobbly and, later, International Brigader in Spain" This does not map very well against the claim that he was in the Royal Navy in 1931, and was arrested for activities relating to a strike in the merchant navy in February 1932.

---

[84] Hopkins JK, '*Into the Heart of the Fire: The British in the Spanish Civil War*', Stanford Press 1998 p408

A member of the Communist Party in Liverpool, he
volunteered for service in Spain in 1936. He listed his political

*International Brigader passport of Albert Cole, Working
Class Movement Library, Salford*

stance as 'Anti-Fascist' on his military documentation rather
than Communist. In Spain his skills as a seaman were put to use
on a torpedo boat rather than on the front line. As such he saw
action disrupting the supply lines to Franco's armies from Italy and
Germany. Hospitalised in 1938 with concussion, he was
discharged from the brigade in 1938 and sent home.

There is a section of the International Brigade exhibition in
Working-Class Movement Library in Manchester which uses
Albert Cole to illustrate how volunteers got to fight in Spain[85].
Cole was also mentioned in an article in the *Liverpool Echo* of
July 1, 1938. In the article Liverpool university students went out
to visit the International Brigaders from Merseyside. While they
were there they were informed by JL 'Jack' Jones that rumours of

---

[85] https://unlockideas.wordpress.com/2014/07/02/albert-cole-
international-brigader-in-the-spanish-civil-war/

Cole's death were greatly exaggerated and that he had communicated with Cole personally.

Cole had two tours of duty before he was finally sent home. He left the CPGB because of the Nazi Soviet pact in 1939

## Grady, Jim Aged 27 in 1932

This biographical portrait is mostly based on Jim Grady's entry in: https://grahamstevenson.me.uk/?s=Grady

Jim Grady was born in Wigan and worked in the mines for 17 years. He was involved in major strikes, becoming victimised because of his trade union activity.

He became involved in unemployed movement activities in the early 1930s, being beaten with batons by the police during unemployment demonstrations. He joined the Communist Party in 1931. The first mention of him in the *Daily Worker* is as an attendee at the funeral of Alex Hermon in 1935

Grady was a student at the International Lenin School in Moscow in 1932 although it is not clear when he graduated or left [86]. He became Communist Party organiser for South East Lancashire and North East Lancashire and later Merseyside in 1938.

## Hedley, Jack aged 42 in 1926

At the height of the general strike, on May 10, 1926, the *Liverpool Echo* reported the arrest of John Hedley, aged 42[87]. At this point Hedley was the leader in the city of the NUWCM. This was the first of many appearances in the paper which resulted from Hedley's activities in the CPGB. Born in Goole in 1885 John (Jack) Frederick Hedley came to the Communist Party via the Socialist Labour Party which he joined in Whitehaven in 1907[88] . He had been a stoker in the navy but was inspired by his

---

[86] McIlroy J, Campbell A, McLoughlin B, Halsread J, *'Forging the Faithful: The British at the International Lenin School'* Labour History Review 2003 68(1):99-128

[87] *Liverpool Echo*, May 10, 1926

[88] Greaves Desmond C, *'Sean O'Hagan' Dies in Liverpool.* Irish Democrat, Nov 1952

recruitment into Socialism to desert and take up revolutionary activity in Belfast. He was one of three socialists who were jailed for four months for staging meetings, declared illegal assemblies by the authorities, during a general strike in the city in 1919. When he was in prison, he embarked on a hunger strike and like the suffragettes before him, he was released under the terms of the 'Cat and Mouse' act. Released from prison he made his way to Sheffield where he resumed his activities with the Socialist Labour Party. Under the act, he was re-arrested in Sheffield and returned to Crumlin Road jail in January 1920. He resumed his hunger strike and was finally released in May. While he was in prison the Socialist Labour Party set up a 'Jack Hedley' defence fund and his wife contributed stories to their paper concerning his fate. After his release he became an organiser for the Irish Transport and General Workers Union. He took on the name 'Sean O'Hagan' and was involved in the setting up of a 'Soviet' in Limerick. In his book 'The Limerick Soviet' Liam Cahill tells

*Jack Hedley, back row and second from right.*

the story of how workers took over a dairy enterprise, hoisted the red flag and declared 'We make butter, not profits'[89]. In May 1921 he was again sent to prison for six months with hard labour for making a seditious speech to sailors in Portsmouth. His trial was held in secret under the provisions of the Emergency Powers Act [90]. Returning to Liverpool he joined the Communist Party and remained a citizen of the city until his death. At the outbreak of the Spanish civil war, he volunteered for service even though he was in his 50s. He appears in this photograph in the back row,

---

[89] Cahill L *The forgotten revolution: the Limerick Soviet.* Orla Kelly publishing, 2019

[90]

https://research.tees.ac.uk/ws/files/4416942/They_will_never_understand_why_I_m_here_British_Marxism_and_the_Irish_Revolution_1916_1923_Sep_2017.pdf

second from the right. He became an official of the painter's union and retained this post until his retirement at 65.

## Hermon, Alex aged 35 in 1936

On March 3, 1936, the front page of the *Daily Worker* carried a large article with the news that Alec (sic) Hermon had died of pneumonia at the age of 35. In the same article Bill Rust talked of the positions of responsibility that Hermon had taken 'at home and abroad'. Hermon was an electrician and ETU activist who had represented the ETU at the TUC. He left London to become the Communist Party organiser in Liverpool. In the same article one AE Scrivens, an ex-comrade from the Southwark area of London paid tribute to Hermon in 'building the Communist Party in that area in the dark days after the general strike'. Although he died in Liverpool, his body was taken back to London, and he was buried at the Kensal Green cemetery in London. On March 5 Everton branch of the Communist Party referred to their gratitude at 'the wonderful assistance given by him to the local during the months he was in this district'.

On March 9, in addition to a tribute from the Lewisham branch of the ETU, the *Daily Worker* published a resolution of the Liverpool local of the Communist Party. '*His death at such an early age was largely due to the exhaustive efforts on behalf of the working class, and we are sure that Alex would desire no better memorial than an increase in the tempo of the building of the Communist Party and the Daily Worker, to which his whole efforts were devoted'*.

Even though the *Daily Worker* reported the death of Alec Hermon, this name varies in the other accounts of his demise. And most references to him use the name Alex. There is more confusion over his name elsewhere. Noreen Branson refers to an 'Alec Herman' from London being expelled from the AUEW in 1931 [91]. The index of her history of the Communist Party also refers to a Herman on the Central Committee of the Communist Party in 1929, but the initial in this case is given as E.

The general impression from the time was that Alec Hermon was a young and enthusiastic officer of the party, well-liked by those who knew him. But it turns out that Hermon was a much more controversial character than this thumbnail would suggest. If indeed Noreen Branson's Herman, E on the party's central committee was in fact Hermon, A then he achieved this grand office in the party at the congress of December 1929. This congress was the second called in 1929. The previous congress was in January of that year. Considerable controversy had broken out in the party over the new 'Class Against Class' policies which at that time were being promulgated by the Comintern. This latter policy had been interpreted by many in the CPGB to mean that the Labour Party and trade union leaderships should be 'ruthlessly exposed' as William Rust put it. Affiliation to the Labour Party was to be abandoned as an aim of the party. Members of unions should be encouraged to withhold their political contributions to Labour. And perhaps most controversially, electors should be advised not to vote for Labour in elections. Against this view stood a faction who regarded this view as too extreme and saw its implementation as being likely to alienate left leaning labourites and trade union allies. They pointed to the rapidly collapsing membership figures of the party as evidence of the isolating tendency of these 'new line' strictures. In January 1929, against

---

[91] Branson N, '*History of the Communist Party of Great Britain 1927-1945*', Lawrence and Wishart, 1985.

the advice of the party leadership, congress delegates elected a central committee sympathetic to the latter point of view including JR Campbell. Also elected was the future party organiser in Liverpool, Frank Bright who was then working as the organiser in Lancashire. But by the time of the December congress opinion in the party had hardened in favour of the new line. The talk was all about the dangers of 'right deviation' and the fall in party membership was attributed not to the harsh rigours of the new line but, on the contrary, to the fact that that the new line was not being pursued with sufficient vigour. JR Campbell retained his seat on the CC by a narrow margin in December but out went Frank Bright. Into the CC came a new batch of Liverpool 'Young Turks' including Leo McGree and Charlie Hoyle, along with Alex Hermon, soon to be from Liverpool.

Almost as soon as he was appointed to the CC, Hermon, along with JR Campbell were dispatched to the Comintern in Moscow as representatives of the CPBG to be indulged in bouts of criticism from Moscow about the developments in the British party. As an opponent of 'right deviationism' as instanced by Campbell, Hermon may well have expected a friendly reception in the Comintern. However, things are never so cut and dried in politics. Despite differences in political leanings, the experienced political operator JR Campbell impressed Comintern officials much more than the enthusiastic young buck Hermon who failed to impress at all and was described as 'dull and incompetent' [92]. By 1930 Hermon was back in London. But this was not to be his last visit to Russia. Between 1932 and 1935 he was listed as being a student at the International Lenin School in Moscow. When he returned to Britain in 1935, he must have gone almost directly to Liverpool to take up the post of organiser, aged 34. He had eighteen more months to live.

### Hoyle, Charlie, aged 28 in 1930

Described in the *Liverpool Echo* in September 1925 as the

---

[92] Thorpe A, '*Comintern 'Control' of the Communist Party of Great Britain, 1920-43*' The English Historical Review , Vol. 113, No. 452 (Jun., 1998), pp.637-662

Liverpool District Organiser of the Communist Party Hoyle was for many years a prominent Communist Party member in the city, and probably a full-time officer following IP Hughes. He was a prolific writer to the local press and engaged in many debates through its letter column. Hoyle stood in the election to be the president of the Amalgamated Engineering Union in 1930 at the age of 28. This would place his date of birth at 1902. Hoyle was elected to the executive of the CPGB at its 11th congress in 1929[93]. In May 1930 he was the district secretary of the Minority Movement[94]. He was a graduate of the International Lenin School in Moscow between 1930-1932, the same years as a subsequent Liverpool organiser, Frank Bright[95]. In the early 1930s Hoyle was giving lectures in the North West on life in the USSR. He wrote occasional articles for the *Daily Worker* . The Dictionary of Labour Biographies mentions Charlie Hoyle as an inspiring character in the education of Edmund Frow who, with his wife Ruth, went on to found the Working-Class Movement Library in Manchester. Frow met Hoyle when he was an engineering steward at the Meccano factory in Edge Lane. Hoyle was said to have been a tutor in the Labour Colleges. By 1935 the *Daily Worker* carried an advert which placed him as an AEU branch secretary in Brixton. He finally settled at RS Stevens engineering in Crystal Palace where he was a steward from 1945 until 1970. He stood again for the presidency of the AEU in 1934 and the post of general secretary in 1945. Later in his life Charlie Hoyle would be an activist in the national Federation of Tenants Associations.

---

[93] Noreen Branson, *History of the Communist Party of Great Britain 1927-1941*, Lawrence and Wishart, 1985
[94] *Daily Worker* May 17, 1930.
[95] Cohen G, Morgan K, *Stalin's Sausage Machine.British Students at the International Lenin School, 1926–37.*
Twentieth Century British History, Vol. 13, No. 4, 2002, pp. 327–355

**Hughes, IP. Cedar Grove. Aged 39 years in 1932 .**

Ieuan Peter Hughes name appears on one of the first advertisements for the Communist Party in Liverpool, one which gives the party's address as 14 Marmaduke Street. There are varying dates given for his birth but the 1901 census gives his age as 4 and his birth date as 1897. Born and raised in North Wales he joined the Independent Labour Party at an early age and at 16 joined the shop workers union in Wrexham. When the first world war broke out, he joined many in the Independent Labour Party who refused to fight. They refused on political rather than moral grounds; refusal to fight in an imperialist conflict. He became the secretary of the No-Conscription Fellowship[96] in Wales. Although their office was in Cardiff, he was arrested in North East Wales. He was imprisoned and eventually was sent to Dartmoor. While he was there another prisoner called Henry Firth, who was a Methodist minister, was given hard labour even though he was clearly unwell. When he died IP Hughes led a strike of all the conscientious objectors [97]. At the inquest it was revealed that Firth was an undiagnosed diabetic [98]. For his role in the strike Hughes was arrested again and sent to another prison. An obituary in the Socialist Worker in 1971 (which reads like an article written by someone known personally to Hughes) suggested that at the end of the war he managed to escape from confinement, and he made his way to Liverpool[99]. Here he made a living as a dockworker. In Liverpool he joined the British Socialist Party and followed the majority of that organisation into the Communist Party of Great Britain in 1920. He became the first Communist Party organiser in

---

[96] https://en.wikipedia.org/wiki/No-Conscription_Fellowship

[97] Eirug, A. . *Opposition to the Great War in north-east Wales*. Transactions of the Denbighshire Historical Society, (2018), 91-105.

[98] Graham JW, '*Conscription and conscience: a history 1916-1919*' Allen and Unwin, 1922 p 321

[99] Hill R, *The Death of IP Hughes- the revolutionary who never gave up*. Socialist Worker, Oct 9, 1971 p 6

the Liverpool District. He was a presence in all the activities of the Communist Party throughout the 1920s. This included participating in protests over unemployment, and he was arrested and tried when these protests turned unruly. He was a defendant in the Islington riot case of 1932, where he gave his profession as 'journalist'. He was active in the Minority Movement and went on to its executive committee at one point. He stood in local elections for the Communist Party. However, he increasingly became at odds with the direction of the Communist Party. By the early 1930s this had come to a head. In 1934 a short item in the *Daily Worker* entitled 'Liverpool Expulsions' reported that IP Hughes and Wilfred Fielding of the Young Communist League had been expelled from the party for an unspecified 'political unreliability'[100]. An obituary in the Socialist Worker suggested that, although the official reason was that he had pursued initiatives in the Minority Movement without consulting the party leadership, he was in fact disenchanted with what he saw as the leadership's slavish loyalty to changes in policy originating in Moscow. Following his expulsion Hughes performed something of an ideological trek. Along with Ben Tillett and Tom Mann he was said to be a pallbearer at dockers union leader and MP James Sexton's funeral in 1938. Early in the 1920s Sexton had been the subject of intense criticism from the Communist Party under Hughes leadership. In the 1935 Liverpool street index Hughes was still listed as a journalist. In the quasi-census of 1939 Hughes gave his occupation as 'political organiser' although it is not specified what this means. There is mention of correspondence in 1939 between Hughes and the founders of the various Trotskyist strands some of which coalesced into the Militant Tendency of the 1980s[101]. On the other hand, the Socialist Worker claimed that he had joined the International Socialists by the time of his death in

---

[100] Liverpool Expulsions. *Daily Worker*, May 18, 1934 p 4.
[101] McIlroy J, Obituary Jimmy Deane *Encyclopaedia of Trotskyism On-Line: Revolutionary History* Vol 8, No 3

1971. Certainly by 1949 he was sharing a platform with his old comrade Jack Braddock in the 1949 local election campaign[102]

## Martinson, Charlie, Oregon Street Bootle. Aged 30 in 1939

In the *Daily Worker* of August 1935, a 'worker correspondent' reported that, after defending himself ably in courts, Charles Martinson was bound over to keep the peace for one year. His appearance in court resulted from a fracas which took place outside the offices of a landlord in Bootle. Six hundred people had turned up to a demonstration and trouble had occurred. Martinson was arrested.

An activist in the Communist Party and the NUWM Martinson who was born in Dublin became a volunteer for the International Brigade in Spain. He was captured on the Madrid front in 1937 and spent six months in a fascist prison, His release was reported in the *Liverpool Echo* [103].

While in Spain, and like George Orwell, he became disillusioned with the Communist Party because of its treatment of the POUM, a non-Stalinist Marxist faction on the republican side. After leaving the Communist Party he remained active in left

---

[102] *Liverpool Echo* May 9, 1949

[103] *Liverpool Echo* '*Bootle wife is overjoyed*' 14 Sept 1937

wing politics and was prosecuted in 1939 for participating in a 'lie down' protest in Bootle on behalf of the NUWM [104].

After WW2 he got a job on the docks and became an early member of the Trotskyist Revolutionary Communist Party (RCP). An article by Jimmy Deane in the Trotskyist newspaper 'Socialist Appeal' of 1945 reports that Martinson was to stand for the RCP in Bootle. This was also reported in the Militant, the paper of the Socialist Workers Party in America[105].

There is a full-page report in the anarchist newspaper about him following a spell working as a miner in St Helens [106].

## INTERNATIONAL NOTES

### England

The English Trotskyists have nominated Comrade Charles Martinson, militant Liverpool dock worker, as the Revolutionary Communist Party candidate for the Mersey Ward, Bootle, in the forthcoming Borough Council elections, according to the Mid - October English Socialist Appeal.

In 1933 Comrade Martinson joined the Communist Party. A year later he was elected organiser of the Bootle unemployed movement. Under his efficient, fighting leadership, the unemployed secured many concessions from the local authorities. Comrade Martinson was also Chief Marshal of the Lancashire Hunger Marchers at that time.

It was in Spain fighting against Franco and Fascism as a member of the International Brigade in 1936 that Comrade Martinson first observed the degeneration of the Communist Party, and its treacherous collaboration with the bosses. Today he is a member of the Trotskyist movement.

With a long record of heroic struggles on behalf of the work-

CHARLES MARTINSON

Koreans were estimated to be laboring as virtual slaves in Japanese factories and mines.

While Major General A. D. Bruce, commander of the 77th Division occupying Hokkaido Island hypocritically proclaims that "No Chinese or Korean's return to the homeland will be delayed a single day because of working in the mines," he has ordered the miners back into the pits at a pay scale of 20 to 66 cents. "Those who produced the most coal have been promised quickest repatriation," reported the Post.

### Nigeria

The main demand of the Nigerian workers in the general strike of last summer was 2 shillings and 6 pence a day minimum wage. The government promised to grant this demand. Now, however, Captain D. H. Holley, head of the Labor Department, has broken this promise, according to a dispatch from London in the Chicago Defender. Instead the government has offered the workers a three pence increase, totally inadequate to meet the steep rise in the cost of living.

Leaders of the Nigerian trade unions called a mass meeting and issued an ultimatum to Governor Sir Arthur Richards that unless the full amount promised, together with back pay, is immediately granted, the general strike will be renewed.

A mass meeting of workers in Lagos unanimously adopted a resolution of "No Confidence in the administration of Richards." The trade unions sent a cable to Prime Minister Attlee and George Hall, Secretary of State for Colonies, threatening a general protest strike unless their demand for the recall of Richards and other high-ranking officials is met.

### Poland

The piece-work system of pay, "the worst form of capitalist exploitation used against the work-

## McGree, Leo 1900 - 1967

Abridged from http://website.lineone.net/~nick-nam...rpoollives.htm:

"A fighter for his class". By Ronnie Williams

*"Over thirty years since his death, Leo McGree is still remembered as a fighter for his class on Merseyside.*

*He was born in 1900 to an Irish father and a Scottish mother. His childhood and youth were spent against the backdrop of the great*

---

[104] *Evening Express*, 'Lie down demonstrators in court' 24 Jan 1939

[105] *The Militant*, paper of the American Socialist Workers Party, 24 Nov 1945

[106] Freedom, '*The strange case of Charlie Martinson*' 8 March 1947

*transport strike on Merseyside in 1911, the senseless slaughter of the war and a decade of industrial unrest. He left school at 14 and tried his hand at numerous jobs before settling as an apprentice joiner. He found work in Sheffield where he met his wife Hetty. It was in Sheffield that he joined the Communist Party. He returned to Liverpool and set up home in Edge Hill. At 21, he was a branch secretary in the Amalgamated Society of Woodworkers. This was at a time when blacklisting of trade union activists was commonplace.*

*During the 20s numerous rank and file publications appeared written by and for building workers, ship builders, and dockers. Leo McGree was arrested for selling one such paper and frogmarched through town to Warren Street Bridewell. He was subsequently released without charge but the papers were confiscated. He was instrumental in ensuring that the Daily Worker survived and arranged for the London train to be met each morning at 04.20. As the Lancashire wholesalers refused to distribute the paper, it was left to Leo and his comrades to cycle around Merseyside and leave copies at newsagents and through letterboxes.*

*Open air public meetings were a feature of the political scene before the advent of television, and speakers would be arranged at various venues throughout the town. On one occasion, a speaker could not make it and Leo was asked to speak to a crowd outside the docks. With a chair for a rostrum, Leo spoke on the Industrial Revolution and the Enclosures Act. An old anarchist encouraged him to continue public speaking which he did until his death. He was a man who loved his class but was not blind to their shortcomings. In one such address, he berated the listeners with 'You fools, you fight each other every 12th of July and 17th of March, but forget about your empty bellies for the rest of the year!'*

*His sharp wit was legendary. After giving a talk about the expropriation of land from the wealthy he was asked by Lord Derby what McGree would give him for his land. 'A receipt' was the riposte. Another time, the Communist Party invited him to speak in Moscow on the plight of Britain's fishing crews. He had prepared six pages and was asked to reduce this to two. He*

*promptly glued the first three sheets together, then the second three, and gave his talk.*

*In 1932, the unemployed of Birkenhead protested and, when attacked by the police, fought back. Leo was in Burnley raising funds for striking cotton workers, but the police were determined to arrest him for his part in the 'riots' in Birkenhead. After evading arrest for several weeks he was caught and beaten up by police after addressing a crowd off Scotland Road. While being cuffed to a plain clothes policeman on the train to Walton Gaol. Other passengers noticed the handcuffs. Leo said in a loud voice, 'I had great difficulty with this chap, but eventually I caught him.' He was sentenced to twenty months imprisonment, which was spent in Strangeways. He asked for a razor and was asked by the prison*

87

*doctor if he had any suicidal tendencies. 'No, only murderous ones' came the reply.*

*As well as being a trade union activist and leader of the unemployed, he was active in the anti-fascist struggle on Merseyside and helped organise a counter demonstration when Oswald Mosley arranged to speak off Queens Drive in Walton.*

*In 1950 Leo McGree was District President of the Confederation of Shipbuilding and Engineering Unions. This was at the height of the anti-communist witch hunts in the USA and Britain. Leo was pilloried in the Daily Express for calling for pay rises for ship builders and a strict ban on overtime. At this time, Leo was also removed from most of the positions he held within the union.*

*It would be easy to pass judgement on Leo McGree with hindsight, but with almost forty years membership of the Communist Party behind him, it was perhaps not surprising that he went along with the decision of the Soviet Union to invade Hungary in 1956. He saw the uprising as a counter-revolution which was how the Soviet Union portrayed it and he was by no means alone in reaching that conclusion. This should in no way detract from his commitment to the struggle for a better world for his class.*

*He carried on the fight for social justice right up until his untimely death in 1967. The funeral proceedings had to be relayed to the huge crowd that gathered outside the chapel at Anfield cemetery. If Leo McGree had his differences with the TUC leadership, he will be remembered as being at one with the rank and file from whatever socialist viewpoint they may have come from."*

### Nield, Jack. 98 Stanley Road. Aged 36 in 1921

In 1921 a well-attended demonstration of the unemployed turned rowdy. Fleeing the batons of the police on St Georges plateau the demonstrators assembly point, a number of the protestors entered and occupied the Walker art gallery. The police followed them and suppressed the occupation. There were 162 arrests. On September 21 the *Yorkshire Post* reported that the local stipendiary magistrate had come back from his annual leave to expedite the legal processing of the alleged unemployed lawbreakers [107]. All the accused respected the terms of their bail and turned up to the police court for their arraignment. The Yorkshire Post reported that all but twelve of the defendants accepted the offer of the authorities to be bound over to keep the peace for one year. Of that twelve, one was Jack Nield. With the others, Nield was accused of unlawful assembly. The Post described Neild's cross examination of the police as 'lengthy and clever'. He was accused of abetting John Meehan who in the opinion of the police had made a speech which was 'considered to be dangerous and amounted to incitement to violence'. The police witness read a one-hundred-word excerpt from Meehan's speech indicating its most inflammatory passages. When asked by Nield if he could take shorthand notes the officer said that he could not. Nield questioned how then he could, under oath, swear to the veracity of his long hand record.

Jack Nield started his electoral career in the brief period between 1920 and 1925 when it was possible to be both a member of the Communist Party and the Labour Party. Increasingly this became an uncomfortable pairing for the Labour Party which put pragmatism before principles, or dogma, depending on the point of view [108]. By 1925 the Communist Party was a proscribed organisation and people suspected of sympathies with it were excluded from the ranks.

In the local elections of 1921 Nield stood against the official Labour candidate James Sexton, who later went on to top a career as a full-time union officer by becoming an MP. In 1921 Nield described himself as a 'Communist' on the ballot and received 43% of the vote to Sexton's 57%. In 1922 Nield described himself as 'Independent Labour' and won, receiving 57% of the vote. By 1925 his vote was down to 16% and this vote had declined again to 0.8% in 1926. In 1922 Nield nominated fellow 'Art gallery siege' defendant Bob Tissyman to be Lord Mayor as he

---

[107] *Yorkshire Post, 'The raid on Liverpool art gallery'* 21 sept 1921

[108] https://grahamstevenson.me.uk/2013/03/17/nield-john/

'represented the public'. When asked whether he in turn should be nominated, Nield replied 'I don't represent the public. I represent the working class'[109].

When Nield was elected to the council as an avowed communist he was accompanied by 200 unemployed workers to his maiden sitting. The *Daily Mail* (Nov 10, 1922) reported that they carried a makeshift coffin with them which bore a wreath made from straw with two top hats on it to mark the fact that he had been placed on the Baths and Burials committee. His entry to the chamber was loudly cheered from the gallery.

In May 1923 the *Liverpool Echo* reported that Nield had secured a post working for the journal '*The Critic*'. This would allow him to 'take advantage of the wide experience he had gained through several phases of his life'. Whether anything came of this appointment is hard to say. But the next time Nield hit the national headlines was in June 1923. The Evening News ran a story headlined 'COMMUNIST COUNCILLOR-Obliged to go into workhouse'. Still unemployed he declared 'We have had to pawn everything, even my wife's wedding ring'. This put his attendance at council meetings at risk, but he asserted that he would sign himself out of the workhouse and reapply after the council meetings.

On September 4, 1924, Nield was in the papers once more. The *Northern Daily Mail* reported him being physically ejected from a city council meeting. He had put forward a motion which deplored the treatment of pedlars and hawkers by the police. The motion was declared out of order by the mayor, but Nield would not let the matter drop. He objected to the charge against the pedlars that their barrows and pitches caused obstruction, when the rich were allowed to park their cars anywhere they wanted. He further questioned the big store owners who professed commitment to capitalist competition when, on request, the police would remove

---

[109] Davies RSW, '*Differentiation in the working class, class consciousness and the development of the Labour Party in Liverpool up to 1939*'
http://researchonline.ljmu.ac.uk/id/eprint/4943/1/261619.pdf

any street trader who set up within sight of their shops. In the end the police intervened and manhandled the councillor out. The Mail reported that many of the, mostly Tory, councillors were by this point shouting 'Put him out!'. Nield, who represented a ward in the Scotland Road area replied, 'Come and try it on, any one of you!'

Neild's final appearance in the press was in 1927. Newly appointed official of the National Unemployed Workers Committee Movement, he responded to a letter that had appeared in the *Echo* from one Mr Longbottom. This letter asserted that the coffers of the committee had been ransacked by the previous incumbent, Jack Hedley. He further asserted that the NUWCM in Liverpool was a fig leaf organisation for the Communist Party. In a long and well-argued response Nield defended Hedley, who had found employment, defended the Communist Party who, he said, fought hardest and longest for the unemployed and countered that the real embezzlers of the unemployed were the landlords, councillors like Mr Longbottom and the administrators of 'relief'.

In 1931 he spoke at a demonstration of 6000 unemployed people on behalf of the NUWM [110]

Nield was advertised as writing for the *Daily Worker* in Feb 1931, he also reported in the *Daily Worker* that he saw McGree 'treated like a murderer' during an arrest for obstruction. In the article he was described as a *Daily Worker* distributor. He was regularly described as a 'guarantor' on contributions to the *Daily Worker*.

### Mrs Annie Walker aged 57 in 1931

Annie Walker was a well-known British Socialist Party member and a foundation member of the CPGB. She was born in Yorkshire and had been in the Social Democratic Federation and early in her life and had been the first secretary of the Socialist Sunday School in New Wortley. During the labour unrest in 1911 she had been imprisoned in Manchester and had been fined after an arrest for making inflammatory speeches during the General

---

[110] *Daily Worker* '6000 demonstrate in Liverpool' 19 Sept 1931

# A WOMAN FIGHTER PASSES

## Death Of Mrs. Annie Walker Of Liverpool

The DAILY WORKER deeply regrets to announce the death of Comrade Mrs. Annie Walker, of Liverpool, in her 57th year. Our comrade died on Sunday, and the funeral takes place to-day, the cortege leaving 30, Thorburn Street, Edge Hill, at 10.45 a.m.

The interment will be at Anfield Cemetery at 11.30 a.m.

Comrade Walker was an old revolutionary, first joining the Social-Democratic Federation in Yorkshire over 30 years ago. She was the first secretary of the Socialist Sunday School at New Wortley.

Her magnificent energy in the fight for the overthrow of capitalism was characteristic of her whole career in the S.D.F., the British Socialist Party, and finally in the Communist Party.

In Manchester, in 1911, she served a term of imprisonment as a result of her revolutionary activities, and during the General Strike of 1926 she was fined for a speech made to the miners at St. Helens.

After the General Strike Comrade Walker was compelled to go into domestic service—the strain of which really killed her—and was much worried that she was therefore unable to continue her various propaganda and organising activities for the Party.

Till her death, however, she was active as a delegate to the Liverpool Trades and Labour Council, fighting for the unemployed on the Court of Referees.

The example of Comrade Annie Walker will inspire us all to yet keener efforts in the cause to which her life was devoted.

Strike in 1926. Following the General Strike poverty forced her to go into domestic service. Throughout, she was a delegate to the Trades Council and represented the council on the court of referees, an appeals tribunal in the unemployment benefits system. Annie Walker died aged 57 in 1931.

# A word about sources

Although I recognise that the profligate use of Wikipedia is not regarded as academic good practice, I have made widespread use of its resources in the study. This is in circumstances where the Wikipedia content is not central to the main subject under discussion.

Even though the Communist Party of Great Britain (CPGB) started as recently as the 1920s, the study of its organisation on Merseyside in its early years is difficult because so few first-hand sources are left. The closer to 1920, the worse this problem becomes. In its early years the party in the region had very few members and fewer resources. Little thought was given to the historical record among members who were convinced that the capitalist dominoes would soon start to fall after the Bolsheviks had tumbled the first pieces in Russia. There are very few internal documents from Merseyside to give an insight into the organisation, membership and thinking of the party in the tumultuous years of the 1920s. More accurately, there are some documents from Liverpool in this period in the CPGB archive at the ever-helpful People's History Museum in Manchester and the Working-Class Movement Library in Salford. But even where local documents exist, in the main they record political statements. There is rarely any comment about branch structure, membership or even the appointment of full-time officers. The party newspapers such as the *Workers Weekly* and the *Workers World* do not cover regional affairs in any detail and where they do, it tends to be in the areas of party strength: the mining areas, and areas populated by engineering works.

With little in the way of internal documents to go on, the local activities of the party are most extensively covered in the local press, notably the *Liverpool Echo*. This is a risky business because the *Echo* was hardly non-partisan in its coverage of party affairs in the 1920s. Its attitude in the period could best be described lying somewhere between mockery and blatant hostility. Its gossip column is frequently expressive of deeply hostile sentiments. But this doesn't mean that its coverage is without merit. The adverts placed by the party for one thing, tell a story. Likewise, the frequent appearance in the letters column of contributions from the party district organisers also give an insight into the minds of the party membership at that time. Reports of court appearances by the leadership of the subdistrict indicate accurately the ages and addresses of the members.

One of the very few reminiscences about the internal life of the party in 1920s Liverpool occurs in the joint biography of the Braddocks, Bessie and Jack, published in the 1960s. By this stage in their careers both the Braddocks had completely travelled the arc from youthful rebellion as leaders of the CPGB in the city to the Communist Party's implacable opponents. Yet their recollections are of some value if sipped with caution, even if it is just for their rarity value.

In January 1930 the CPGB launched the *Daily Worker*. It's entire archive is available online and is searchable by keywords and date. This makes the research of the period in Liverpool more straightforward, at least as reported in the pages of the paper. Many of the articles in the paper draw little distinction between news and comment to propaganda and wishful thinking and it is wise to treat them with healthy scepticism. For example, there are many stories which tell of large numbers of new recruits to the party and the impression is easily created of a party which was growing steadily. In fact, while it may have been true that there were regular transfusions of new blood into the organisation, the party always found the simultaneous haemorrhage of members hard to control. Nevertheless, the news section of the paper's coverage of the city's affairs gives some insight about events and the people involved in them. Arguably, the reader is on more solid ground looking elsewhere in the paper. Particularly useful was the small adverts section. These adverts recounted where and when meetings took place and who would be present at them. The copy writers may have exaggerated the numbers attending a meeting, but the adverts recorded simply that the meeting took place. Even if nobody attended, someone thought it worthwhile to place the advert. The trends in the advertised events therefore give an interesting picture of what was going on in the city for party members. The adverts also give addresses to which people could attend for meetings and activities. contributors. Jack Nield, Liverpool's 'legacy' communist councillor, is one of these. His name appears as a guarantor of collection money until the mid 1930s, then he disappeared from view.

# Bibliography, further reading and some on line sources

## Web based sources:

- Imperial War Museum:
https://www.iwm.org.uk
- For the history of conscientious objectors in WW1, the website 'The Men Who Said No':
https://menwhosaidno.org
- For a general source of information and documents I have made heavy use of:
https://www.marxists.org
- For an account of the Walker Art Gallery siege, the George Garrett archive;
https://www.georgegarrettarchive.co.uk
- The Graham Stevenson website of biographies of left wingers who would otherwise have been lost to history:
https://grahamstevenson.me.uk
- Interesting account of the life of Ben Bradley:
https://www.open.ac.uk/researchprojects/makingbritain/content/ben-bradley
- When the king passed by the swastikas in Rodney Street:https://bygoneliverpool.wordpress.com/2020/12/06/a-nazi-consulate-in-rodney-street/

- Pat Ayers  on Mary Bamber in '*Free Radical*'
Nerve 9, Autumn 2006
https://web.archive.org/web/20070224090102/http://www.catalystmedia.org.uk/issues/nerve9/bamber_mary.php
- Background material about Ireland and the
British left:
https://research.tees.ac.uk/ws/files/4416942/They_will_never_understand_why_I_m_here_British_Marxism_and_the_Irish_Revolution_1916_1923_Sep_2017.pdf
- The influence of religious sectarianism on
labour politics: Davies RSW, '*Differentiation in the working class, class consciousness and the development of the Labour Party in Liverpool up to 1939*'
http://researchonline.ljmu.ac.uk/id/eprint/4943/1/261619.pdf

## Newspapers:
The main source of material from the Liverpool press came from the British Newspaper Archive:
https://www.britishnewspaperarchive.co.uk

The *Daily Worker* proved more of a problem but the British Online Archive https://microform.digital/boa/ was invaluable for both the Daily Worker and the publications of the British Union of Fascists. A complicating factor was that I had to use my University of Liverpool alumnus card to access them in one of their libraries.

## Books
- Graham JW, '*Conscription and conscience: a history 1916-1919*' Allen and Unwin, 1922
-

- James Klugmann, *History of the Communist Party of Great Britain, Vol 1,* Lawrence and Wishart, London 1968
- Morgan K, Cohen G, Flinn A, *'Communists and British Society 1920-1991'*, Orem Press, 2007
- VI Lenin *Left Wing Communism an Infantile Disorder,* 1920
- Branson N, *'History of the Communist Party of Great Britain 1927-1945'*, Lawrence and Wishart, 1985.
- Lees A, *Liverpool The Hurricane Port* Mainstream Publishing, 2011
- McLoughlin, B: *Left to the wolves: Irish victims of Stalinist terror.* Irish Academic Press, 2007
- Arnison, Jim *Leo McGree: What a man, what a fighter.* Union of Construction and Allied Trade Technicians. 1980
- Frow E, Frow R, *'Frank Bright: Miner, Marxist and Communist 1891- 1944'* North West History Group of the Communist Party
- Hopkins JK, *'Into the Heart of the Fire: The British in the Spanish Civil War'*, Stanford Press 1998
- Martin R, *'Communism and the British Trade Unions 1924-1933'* Clarendon Press, 1969
- Belchem J (ed) *'Liverpool 800'*, Liverpool University Press 2006
- Stephen F Kelly *'Idle hands, clenched fists'* Spokesman books, 1987
- Worley, Matthew (1998) *Class against class: the Communist Party of Great Britain in the third period, 1927-1932* https://eprints.nottingham.ac.uk/11061/1/285474.pdf
-

- Braddock B, Braddock J, *'The Braddocks'* Macdonald, 1963
- Cahill L *The forgotten revolution: the Limerick Soviet.* Orla Kelly publishing, 2019

## Archives:
- First and foremost, the Liverpool Records Office with its searchable online catalogue https://liverpool.gov.uk/libraries/archives-family-history/archive-catalogue/
- Labour History Archive and Study Centre: https://phm.org.uk/collection/labour-history-archive-study-centre/

## Journal articles:
- Wallis, M. *Pageantry and the Popular Front: Ideological Production in the 'Thirties.* New Theatre Quarterly, 1994 *10*(38), 132-156
- Greaves Desmond C, *'Sean O'Hagan' Dies in Liverpool.* Irish Democrat, Nov 1952
- Thorpe A, *'Comintern 'Control' of the Communist Party of Great Britain, 1920-43'* The English Historical Review , Vol. 113, No. 452
- Eirug, A. . *Opposition to the Great War in north-east Wales.* Transactions of the Denbighshire Historical Society, (2018),
- Cohen G, Morgan K, *Stalin's Sausage Machine.British Students at the International Lenin School, 1926–37.* Twentieth Century British History, Vol. 13, No. 4, 2002

www.ingramcontent.com/pod-product-compliance
Ingram Content Group UK Ltd.
Pitfield, Milton Keynes, MK11 3LW, UK
UKHW041319260625
6602UKWH00014B/172

9 798336 328295